Recollections

of the late Fleet Admiral

CHESTER W. NIMITZ

as given by members of his immediate family

U. S. Naval Institute
Annapolis, Maryland

1970

Preface

These manuscripts are the result of a series of tape-recorded interviews conducted by John T. Mason, Jr., Director of the Oral History Office in the U. S. Naval Institute, during 1969 and 1970 with members of the Nimitz family:

    Rear Admiral Chester W. Nimitz, Jr., USN (Ret.)
    Catherine Nimitz Lay and her husband, CAPT
      James T. Lay, USN (Ret.)
    Sister M. Aquinas Nimitz, O.P.

Only minor emendations and corrections have been made by the participants. The reader is asked to bear in mind, therefore, that he is reading a transcript of the spoken, rather than the written, word.

These interviews are part of a series dealing with the late Fleet Admiral Chester W. Nimitz and were intended for use in the preparation of a biography of the Fleet Admiral.

DECLARATION OF TRUST

The undersigned does hereby appoint and designate as his (her) Trustee herein, the Secretary-Treasurer and Publisher of the United States Naval Institute to perform and discharge the following duties, powers, and privileges in connection with the possession and use of a certain taped interview between the undersigned and the Oral History Department of the United States Naval Institute.

(1) As an <u>Open</u> transcript it may be read (or the tape audited) by qualified researchers upon presentation of proper credentials as determined by the Trustee. In the case of interviews about the late Fleet Admiral C. W. Nimitz, it is intended that first use of the material shall be made by the biographer of the Fleet Admiral, Professor E. B. Potter, and the Naval Institute is authorized to deal with the material in this fashion.

(2) It is expressly understood that in giving this authorization, I am in no way precluded from placing such restrictions as I may desire upon use of the interview at any time during my lifetime, nor does this authorization in any way affect my rights to the copyright of any literary expressions that may be contained in the interview.

Witness my hand and seal this ___ day of _____ 19__

I hereby accept and consent to the foregoing Declaration of Trust and the powers therein conferred upon me as Trustee.

DECLARATION OF TRUST

The undersigned does hereby appoint and designate as his (her) Trustee herein, the Secretary-Treasurer and Publisher of the United States Naval Institute to perform and discharge the following duties, powers, and privileges in connection with the possession and use of a certain taped interview between the undersigned and the Oral History Department of the United States Naval Institute.

(1) As an Open transcript it may be read (or the tape audited) by qualified researchers upon presentation of proper credentials as determined by the Trustee. In the case of interviews about the late Fleet Admiral C. W. Nimitz, it is intended that first use of the material shall be made by the biographer of the Fleet Admiral, Professor E. B. Potter, and the Naval Institute is authorized to deal with the material in this fashion.

(2) It is expressly understood that in giving this authorization, I am in no way precluded from placing such restrictions as I may desire upon use of the interview at any time during my lifetime, nor does this authorization in any way affect my rights to the copyright of any literary expressions that may be contained in the interview.

Witness my hand and seal this 1st day of May 1970

Catherine N. Lay
James J. Lay

I hereby accept and consent to the foregoing Declaration of Trust and the powers therein conferred upon me as Trustee:

Secretary-Treasurer and Publisher

DECLARATION OF TRUST

The undersigned does hereby appoint and designate as his (her) Trustee herein, the Secretary-Treasurer and Publisher of the United States Naval Institute to perform and discharge the following duties, powers, and privileges in connection with the possession and use of a certain taped interview between the undersigned and the Oral History Department of the United States Naval Institute.

(1) As an <u>Open</u> transcript it may be read (or the tape audited) by qualified researchers upon presentation of proper credentials as determined by the Trustee. In the case of interviews about the late Fleet Admiral C. W. Nimitz, it is intended that first use of the material shall be made by the biographer of the Fleet Admiral, Professor E. B. Potter, and the Naval Institute is authorized to deal with the material in this fashion.

(2) It is expressly understood that in giving this authorization, I am in no way precluded from placing such restrictions as I may desire upon use of the interview at any time during my lifetime, nor does this authorization in any way affect my rights to the copyright of any literary expressions that may be contained in the interview.

Witness my hand and seal this __1st__ day of __May__ 19_70_.

Sister M. Aquinas Nimitz, O.P.

I hereby accept and consent to the foregoing Declaration of Trust and the powers therein conferred upon me as Trustee:

Secretary-Treasurer and Publisher

Interview with Rear Admiral Chester W. Nimitz, Jr.
and Mrs. Nimitz (Joan) by John T. Mason, Jr.
New Caanan, Connecticut April 14, 1969

Q: Admiral, I can't tell you how happy I am to be with you tonight in your lovely home, and I have been anticipating your conversation, your recollections about your noted father. He has been -- it has been thought that he was not very much interested in recording his recollections, his memoirs; that, for whatever reason, this was something that he shunned. Would you begin by talking about this, perhaps, and your knowledge of him and his reasons for having an attitude of this sort?

Admiral Nimitz: Well, I think it has perplexed all of his children, in any case, this gradually revealed reluctance to participate in any active manner in the recording of his memoirs, because to us, knowing him as a jovial raconteur, and a man who used to love to tell stories about his childhood in Texas, (many of them I've decided are apochryphal), it would have seemed the ideal pastime during his retirement years.

However, the succession of biographies of military and political figures, following, some as they were alive, others as they died off, from World War II began to make clear the very thing that Dad wanted to avoid for himself, and that was, to create in the minds of any living close relative, or the individual himself, of anybody with whom he served a feeling of being criticized, or revealed in some inadequate capacity, because Dad just felt that no purpose was served by in any way bringing unhappiness to those that had served with him or those that were close to those who had served with him. As, for instance, occurred with respect to most everybody that General Montgomery referred to, in one way or another.

Q: Because he had a fairly acid tongue.

Nimitz: Yes, and one might suspect that perhaps General Montgomery was becoming petty, senile and vicious, which I doubt -- which my father in any case I'm sure felt was not what he would have said about those same people during the period of his active leadership.

Q: Well, was this attitude on your father's part, as it developed in his later years, merely a continuation of an attitude he'd always had?

Nimitz: Yes. I think you're very perceptive. The reason that Dad -- the charisma that Dad had for people was his ability -- and I don't quite know how he did it, but he did it -- his ability to communicate the fact that he truly only saw the good in people. I always considered it a weakness. I knew many people in whom he had great confidence and for whom he had high regard that really didn't merit or warrant such admiration. But they probably didn't know that Dad had anything but the highest regard, and I guess it's a fact of life that humans react to the good that people see in them, and not to the bad. Literally, that was the primary facet of his leadership.

If you'll recall, probably the most notable single incident people in general recall historically is that when he finally got himself organized in Oahu, within two or three days after arriving there following his succession to Admiral Kimmel's job, he called in Admiral Kimmel's staff and said words to the effect that he was changing nobody, he had great faith in them, and let's get on with the job. And this was very typical of his approach to things. And I'm sure that every one of those guys increased in his own estimation of himself about 25 percent and therefore became extraordinarily dedicated.

Q: Up to that moment standing in fear and trembling of what would happen?

Nimitz: Absolutely. Funnily enough, incidentally, I never could understand how he was so confident, and he was, that he was going to win the war in Japan, because he also learned and expressed many times to me the greatest of admiration for the great Japanese leaders against whom he fought.

Q: Well, was there anything in this attitude of his -- I mean, a sort of a knowledge that he had some vision of the truth, and therefore it was going to prevail?

Did he have any concept of a pattern of life that would unfold if one persisted?

Nimitz: Well, you know, I really don't know, but he used to use an expression with me that I felt wasn't a great deal of help philosophically in my own life, and I -- but it apparently guided him, and he used it for me many times, and it was, "Chester" --

Let me just preface it by saying that one of the expressions that he admired greatly was one of Vannevar Bush's called "illigitimus non carborundum" which means as you probably know, translated from the Latin, "Don't let the bastards grind you down." The philosophy behind this Dad absolutely adhered to, and that was, do all you can to influence events, as you can properly do, and beyond that, don't let the course of events derange your own thinking, if they're beyond your power to influence.

Nimitz - 5

This ability to say "I have done everything I can properly do to influence the course of events, as I am supposed to do," and then let the chips fall where they may, I believe is the factor that contributed to what many people noted in him, an almost extraordinary serenity.

Another way of putting that, to go back to your question regarding, did he have a philosophy, is that he frequently said to me, "Chester, remember, in the long run, " -- and I emphasize that he emphasized, "in the long run," -- "People get what they deserve." And it was his abiding conviction that the right, the righteous, the side of the right, the side of the men of good will would inevitably triumph always over -- and he liked that expression, and I do too. I think it fits all sorts of cases, that men of good will will triumph over men of other than gxxxxx good will --

Q: -- of evil import --

Nimitz: -- well, maybe it's petty will, but at any rate it isn't good will.

Q: This inevitably leads me to a question about his religious convictions, because you're bordering on this most certainly in terms of destiny and providence and design.

Nimitz: I don't think Father, if the truth be known, believed in a life hereafter. I think he realized, and in many of his speeches or declarations he would refer to the Almighty or some other religious aspect, but I think he did it in deference to those people who he realized leaned on it and set great store by it. I think he was himself sufficiently self-assured and felt that good was enough unto itself, so that that was an end in itself, and I honestly don't believe that Dad was what you might call a religious person, if being religious means adhering to any particular doctrine of any kind. He was a great believer in the Golden Rule. I've heard Dad say to my mother, "Please be sure the children understand that " — This came up, I remember, one night, as a boy, when somebody had come to the door selling something, and Mother was complaining at supper about this disreputable looking character coming to the door to sell something, and I remember my father being quite exercised and saying, "Darling, don't ever deprecate or have anything but a correct feeling for a person who is trying to make an honest living. That's all a man can do." He was very sincere about it.

Q: Would you say something about the religious atmosphere in the family, in which he grew up? Because I think a man necessarily reflects something of his early training and atmosphere. This helps to mold him as a person.

Nimitz: Yes, and I honestly can't say, because I don't know of my

Nimitz - 7

own knowledge at all. I think that to find that out, you would have to go and talk to his sister Dora, his half-sister Dora or his sister-in-law Louisa Nimitz. I have no idea. I suspect that all of these Germans of the river country and hill country of Texas were straitlaced Lutherans, but I honestly don't know of my own knowledge. I do know that in our own family, Father and Mother were not church goers. They made us as children go to Sunday School. I think they did it feeling that they were going to equip us with the ability to then make a decision as we chose. Most of the children went to Catholic elementary schools purely because they were the better schools in the areas we were in. And we've always had friends who were Catholic nuns, priests, ministers, but Dad and Mother themselves did not go to Church at all.

Q: Tell me about your father as a father in the home, his attitude toward his children, what he did to help and inspire them.

Nimitz: Let me say in the first place, Father was a completely dedicated naval officer. And I think such leadership and influence as he did exert in the home, and mind you, in the days we were brought up it was certainly largely an upbringing by the mother because the father was away a good deal of the time -- his method was simply the same method he used everywhere else, to express sublime confidence in the dedication and right thinking

Nimitz - 8

point of view on the part of his children, and of their understanding of the almost necessity of doing well at what they undertake. It certainly was not a close personal kind of a -- this is the way you do things because in the long run that's the way you succeed. It was a considerably more formal sort of standard setting.

I really think that the Navy consumed an extraordinary percentage of his thoughts and energies.

Q: To a greater degree than other naval officers in his own bracket?

Nimitz: Oh, I think so, not to all others, by any manner of means, but certainly to the great percentage, the great average. Any way you want to look at it. You know, a rather indicative thing-- I was a midshipman, I think, and I can't remember the circumstance but I was riding on a bus somewhere in Washington, D.C. This must have been 1935 or '36, when Dad was the Assistant Chief of Naval Personnel, I think then called Assistant Chief of Bureau of Navigation. And I asked him pointblank, "Pop, where do you expect to get in the Navy and how do you expect to get there?"

And Dad said, "Well, you know, what I expect to get of course is I'd like to be the Chief of Naval Operations. And how I get there, " -- I can't remember clearly his answer, but I can certainly paraphrse it. I'm sure it was his standard pattern -- "to do everything you do well, and you will get what you deserve." That basic philosophy of his. He did make the observation that I thought was quite intuitive, that --

" Let me say one thing. I do believe that we are going to have a major war, with Japan and with Germany, and that the war is going to start by a very serious surprise attack and defeat of US armed forces, and that there is going to be a revlusion on the part of the political power in Washington against all of those in command at sea, and they're going to all be thrown out, though it won't be their fault necessarily. And I wish to be in a position of sufficient prominence so that I will then be considered as one to be sent to sea, because that to me appears one route."

And of course that's precisely what happened. He happened to be the Chief of Bureau of Navigation on his next tour of shore duty, when Pearl Harbor did happen, and there he was.

Q: This involves proper timing, too.

Nimitz: Oh, well, I think the timing was fortuitous. He might well have been at sea himself. The timing was fortuitous. But at least he did recognize the virtue of the timing.

Q: To refert again to his philosophy in terms of his children, and others, in expecting them to rise to the occasion and do the best that was in them -- did he then engage in any kind of reward when you met his expectations?

Nimitz: I don't think so. I honestly feel that his standards were sufficiently high and he expected, he exuded this confidence in his subordinates, that in his professional life he could cope wit and tolerate a less than 100 percent performance. I honestly believe in his personal life, he really couldn't. He just damned well expected it, and anything less would have been cause for some other kind of reaction.

Q: You say in his personal life; does this also involve his children, his family?

Nimitz: That's what I mean. In his personal life I feel -- of course, it's much easier for him to see disastrous circumstance in his son than in his daughters.

Q: The emotional --

Nimitz: Yes, emotionally. And I don't think there ever was any concept of reward. It was a concept of , how could we bear anything but? Let me give you a good example. Some four or five months after World War II had been going, I got a letter from Mother saying, "Now, your Father and I would absolutely wish to pray for your safety and life all the time." I was in

Nimitz - 11

submarines. "But above all we expect you to do your duty "—this, this and this, and this was so engraved in the Old Man, I'm sure he'd discussed this with Mother and just wanted to be damned sure I'd get the picture.

Q: Now, in thinking of his subordinates in the Navy, he himself told me of his manner of making appointments, especially during the War in the Pacific, his technique of having men come in and report on the South Pacific, where they'd been on duty and so forth. He naturally wanted to know, but he also wanted to size them up and make sort of a mental notation that this man would measure up in a certain job when it developed. So there was something more than just an expectation that someone would measure up. There was a very shrewd assessment of his ability to begin with.

Nimitz: Yes. And I think Dad tolerated some things in others he wouldn't tolerate in his own family. Coming back to this biographical -- of course, one of the outstanding examples of somebody that he never wanted to be in a position of criticizing, but could scarcely write without saying something that might be deemed as critical, was Admiral Halsey, over the Leyte Gulf business. Dad, I'm sure, in his own mind, considers himself as close and warm a personal friend of Admiral Halsey's as he could possibly be. And the fact that Halsey made an error in judgment, in not leaving Task Force 34 or whatever his surface forces were off San Bernardino Straits and went north, was a very

Nimitz - 12

human failing. The kind of failing that wouldn't necessarily destroy the personal affection between them, but which I am sure made Dad resolve that thereafter, on the jobs that had to be — and my father made this point to me — that had to be done, for which there could be no failure, he would take Spruance. On the jobs that required the flair and the publicity and the marvelous hoopla and esprit de corps aspects, he'd take Halsey.

Q: Could that have been back of this shifting of emphasis?

Nimitz: Oh, absolutely . Absolutely. Where there was a landing, from then on, like Okinawa or any of those places where the forces had to do their job and not be lured off by anything, Spruance was the boy. On the carrier sweeps of the South China Sea, where it was blow 'em up and shoot 'em up , and raise the morale of the Navy and so forth, that was Halsey. Air raids on Japan, that's Halsey — we're not going to invade it.

Q: This was the master strategist, then, wasn't it?

Nimitz: Yes. Incidentally, Dad — another funny thing he used to tell me. I never quite understood how he may have used it , but I remember him telling me once, when I was particularly upset by some person in the Navy I felt was incompetent and so forth,

Nimitz - 13

Dad said, "It just never pays you to make a frontal attack on an individual. He has adherents. He has led a life that has built up certain supports for him" and so forth and so on, and that the correct way to handle a person who was flatly obstructing your proper accomplishment, whatever the purpose is, is to continue to be extraordinarily polite, and don't reveal to him your purpose, and at all times be slowly removing the rug from under him.

So Dad did understand some of the more subtle aspects of coping with adversaries. As for instance ––

Q: –– yes, could you give me an illustration of this?

Nimitz: Yes, well, I don't quite know what the illustration is. I know that Dad had an adversary; when World War II ended, Dad felt that he should, by all normal courses of events, if promotion in the Navy was to follow a logical pattern, should become the Chief of Naval Operations. I think it was Forrestal who was at that time Secretary of the Navy, shortly to become Secretary of Defense, if he wasn't already Secretary of Defense. I think he was Secretary of the Navy. And for some strange reason Forrestal wanted, I gather, to promote some reserve naval officer who'd been the President's aide or something. His name began with R. I can't remember his name. Probably a very able guy, but the fact remains –– I remember my father flying back to Washington on a trip, and our seeing him in

New London, and him saying that he just finally had to say to Forrestal that there just is no answer to putting anybody else in that job, "because if you don't put me in that job, after all, I'm only --" whatever his age was, 57 or so -- "I will be the greatest white elephant flag officer the Navy ever had."

Dad understood what his power was, his personal -- the personal adherents he had in the Navy -- and wasn't at all above leaning on it, when the time came to in fact accomplish something that he felt was absolutely essential for the Navy's interests, that it would destroy any idea that the Navy wasn't a venal political place, to have somebody other than himself become Chief of Naval Operations at that time. And he became Chief of Naval Operations. He was given the appointment for two years, and at the end of two years he was asked to stay on by, I guess it was President Truman, and he then did not choose to. He'd made his point. Incidentally, he was asked by Truman to come back, after he'd been in retirement for either two or four years, I forget which it was. But as he said, that would be the most ridiculous thing, from the point of view of the good of the service.

Q: That again would not be playing the game.

Nimitz: Yes. He was asked to come back when Admiral Sherman died. Dad was a great admirer of Admiral Sherman's and a good friend of his

Nimitz - 15

And it would not help the service. Dad was absolutely all service. I used to ask him how he could bear not to get out into private industry, or into a university job. (He was offered the presidency of UCLA, I know, for one.) And you know, really completely engross himself in another life. But he had this very strong feeling that he represented the Navy to a lot of people who had lost relatives in the Pacific War, and that it would somehow undermine their feeling for the Navy and so forth, if the man who had been the naval commander, under whom their relative had served, acquired an image as other than that naval commander. This was very strongly in his mind, you know.

I used to say, "Dad, for God's sake, why don't you do it? If you don't want the money, give it to your children." Because he was offered all sorts of (to us) ludicrous sums.

Q: You felt, "you'd performed your duty to your country, now do something for yourself."

Nimitz: Yes, and his answer was always, "Yes, but --" we came to understand by various ways of his speaking that he valued and felt was a requirement, as a matter of fact, of the job in which he'd found himself, that he maintain that image until he died, for whatever comfort it was or satisfaction of relatives of people who had died.

Q: No matter what sacrific might be involved.

Nimitz: Right. Dad never had any concept of making a sacrifice insofar as his family was concerned, because as I have pointed out, he had absolutely sublime confidence in his family. A circumstance that I must confess I think my mother feels represented a failure perhaps on her part, or she used to think this, was the fact that my youngest sister, after going to a Dominican convent and I guess -- no, she went to a Dominican convent through high school and then to Stanford University -- elected to become a Catholic, in a family, as I pointed out, very no

Q: -- not denominational--

Nimitz: Not denominational, in any case. And Mother I think was very upset. And I'm quite confident it never bothered my Father at all. I'm sure Father's attitude always was, "Look, if Mary is happier doing that, I can't understand why anybody is moaning and groaning." It certainly is a worthwhile life. She's a teaching nun, and she'll go on and get a doctor's degree. She seems to be sublimely happy. Perhaps she's the most successful.

Q: The emphasis was on her productivity.

Nimitz: Absolutely.

Q: Which she was able to accomplish, with her scientific career.

Nimitz - 17

Going back to the point you made, about his ability to take a long range point of view about something, not to make a frontal attack on a man, can you think of this in terms of his relations with Congress -- which he must have had?

Nimitz: Yes. I really think his relations with Congress must have been extraordinary. Dad was absolutely obsessed with the necessity for civilian control of the armed forces. He never had any other point of view. He had a very high regard for all public servants, and he was most meticulous about any testimony or opinions that he gave before Congress. And I can't say this because I was ever there, but my guess is that he always made an absolutely first class impression on Congress. He was very humble in his personal attitude, so he wouldn't have approached Congress as an overweeningly egotistical brass, for example. I know Mr. Vinson absolutely was crazy over Dad, and I think you might ask Mr. Vinson some day. I think it would be very interesting.

Q: I'm making an effort to reach him. I don't know whether I can. Did he continue, in spite of his heavy obligations, did he always continue to be very much interested in your every activity, as his son?

Nimitz: I wouldn't say it that way, no. I think his concern would have been persistent -- would have been -- his persistent

Nimitz - 18

concern always would have been with a lack of success on the part of his son, and had I been having troubles, I think he would have had considerable more interest or active participation than he ever did. And I think the reason he never did is because he never really had any problem with me, other than paying medical bills. I think he was much more comfortable with a more formal military relationship than with a close personal father and son relationship, which we certainly never did have.

Q: Now, I found a reference in some biographical account of him, in 1942, when he got involved so heavily in the Pacific. The reference was to this effect: that he joined in the Pacific his only son, Lt. Chester Nimitz. This is probably the wrong emphasis?

Nimitz: Absolutely. Absolutely. As a matter of fact, I was somewhere in the Dutch East Indies when I learned that he'd relieved Kimmel, and I sent him a telegram, a cable saying, "Under no circumstances make a move without talking to me." He didn't see the humor of that at all.

Q: You made the point that your father had something of the attitude of, "You're on your own."

Nimitz: Yes, I think the way I put it -- and I think it's the fair and also the more favorable way -- is that Dad had probably the most highly developed sense of duty, as a public servant, and devoted himself first, foremost and always to that aspect of his life, and perhaps secondly to his wife. I believe the children were a natural outgrowth of marriage, and he might have said something, said other words, but my guess is that his basic understanding or belief was, the children were expected to perform and conform and enhance the stature of the family, and so long as they did and were not delinquents, really, that was pretty much the responsibility of the father.

I think maybe the fact is that Dad was really away a tremendous amount of time, so that when he did come home, all of us children understood absolutely and instinctively from our mother that by golly, we made the time he was at home a relatively -- he'd contest this, I'm sure, but by our lights it was relatively serene. It was far more serene than when we were with Mother alone!

Q: When you stress his devotion to duty, was this a sense of duty highly developed at all times in his career, or was it something that came to fruition in wartime?

Nimitz: Oh, no. Absolutely, and my mother would bear this out, he had it, I'm sure, after being in the Naval Academy one week. To him -- let me say, going to the Naval Academy from his background was simply one of the most marvelous things that could happen to a person, and he was immediately loyal to this fantastic government that had offered him this opportunity, and he never lost that point of view, at all.

Q: Now, after his retirement— I suppose one couldn't term it that, because a fleet admiral never retires —

Nimitz: But that's the best description of the circumstance after he left being CNO.

Q: Yes. After that, was there any relaxation in this rigid adherence to duty, vis-a-vis family?

Nimitz: Oh, yes. Yes, I think so. I think he became far more personally interested in the affairs of his family. I think that's a good observation of yours. He did. And not only that, but he also became, I believe, more unbiased perhaps, or unpreconditioned, in his ability to look at the Navy and the Defense Department and the government from a distance, and perhaps be less unquestioningly accepting.

Just let me give you an example. In 1950, I was — I had just had command or left command of a submarine and was going to the Armed Forces Staff College, and at that time, I had become convinced that I simply did not want to spend the rest of my life in the Navy. I'd led a Navy junior's life, and then I'd been in the Navy since 1932, going to the Naval Academy, and it was now 1950. I'd never stopped moving from pillar to post, and I wanted to do something different. And I resigned from the Navy, or tried to, and Dad really opposed it. I believe had he not opposed it, I could have pulled it off, but -- under the guise that the Korean War was starting, they wouldn't let me out. As a matter of fact they were at least flattering enough to say, "You're the first person that we are not going to let resign, and we're allowing no further resignations."

Subsequently in 1956, when I informed him that this time I was going to apply for retirement from the Navy, he not only-- and I asked him that he not oppose it or in any way interfere with it -- he said no, as long as I would agree not to make a great big thing about looking for a job and accepting a job before I actually submitted a retirement request, he would help in fact, he really felt it was the right thing to do. I'm not quite sure why he felt it was the right thing to do, but I think it is associated with what Eisenhower now refers to as the "military industrial complex" -- that the Pentagon, he felt, had become greatly overmanned with civilians, ~~greatly overmanned~~, the status of military people was unsatisfactory, admirals were acting as messenger boys in the Pentagon, -- he was distressed with the type of weaponry, impersonal rockets, air to air missiles, air to ground missiles and intercontinental missiles. And I felt -- I just feel he felt that the kind of person required by the armed forces was no longer the kind of person required for -- that he had felt he had tried to be when he was in the armed forces. In some senses this can be construed as perhaps not staying with the advance of time. I understand what he said. I've made the point many times that the Navy lost its glamor for me when they invented the aircraft carrier, because when I had gone to the Naval Academy, the Battle of Jutland was still the last great romantic sea battle, and carrier warfare sort of really eliminated all this. And I think in a sense this modern age of rockets and mass bombings and so forth disturbed him. It involved too many civilians. I'm not talking about civilian direction, it involved too many civilian casualties. It was no longer the exercise of military force to gain national ends against somebody else's military force, but a pretty cold blooded business.

Finally, when I did get out, he said, "I'm glad you did get out. I think it's high time."

But again, I'm sure he had absolutely sublime confidence that there was no problem. You get out, and with your background and training in the Navy you're bound to be successful in civilian life.

Q: As a corollary to what you're saying about his attitude toward the Navy as it came to be, the whole defense mechanism, the Navy had ceased to be the close knit family unit it once was.

Nimitz: Yes. Well, I can put it another way. I was reminded of the fact, after the 1950 debacle, when they wouldn't let me out -- with the fact that during his entire career, he had two jobs, to my knowledge, in which he was not the commander. At one time he was the assistant chief of staff to the Commander-in-Chief of the United States Fleet. That's when Admiral S.S. Robinson was the admiral. And Dad I know was the apple of Admiral Robinson's eye. Admiral Robinson was always one of the greatest of family friends, and Susie, or whatever his wife's name was -- delightful people. And one other time when he was the exec of a battleship, way way way back. You know, either one of those jobs today would be considered absolutely first class jobs. Those were the two also-ran jobs he had. Every other job, he was in complete command of something. When he graduated from the Naval Academy, he went out to command a gunboat as a past midshipman, and from then on he was always in command. My God, I used to sit and correct enlisted men's training courses, as an ensign on the Indianapolis, and think, "This is just not the most glamorous damned pastime in the world."

He never really, I think, understood that part of it, but he sensed that, when he finally said in his opinion I did probably the right thing. I had the peculiarly unique vantage point of seeing a man become the Chief of Naval Operations, after being in a job which normally would be pure happenstance in a major war, and deciding I did not wish my future to be such that I was

— in that position, at that age in life. He was still tremendously dependent ₍financially₎ upon the mercies of a democracy, which are very tender mercies to be thrown on, and mercies with very short memories.

Q: Rather fickle at times, public opinion.

I recall once talking with Admiral Walter Anderson, who knew your father and who told me, and it was a vivid recollection with him — this was after World War I, somewhere in that period of the late '20s or early '30s, when the Navy was really in the doldrums — Admiral Anderson said that he was present with your father one time when a very enticing offer in the business field was proferred to your father, and that he was tempted to consider it. It would have meant the termination of his naval career. Now, I brought this up to your father when I saw him, and he denied it with great force.

Nimitz: He's wrong. I don't know what his motives were for denying it, but certainly my mother would say that he was crazy, because that name is what struck us, and it is a funny thing, because I believe the job that Admiral Anderson must have been referring to was some position with a company, of all things, called the Castoria company. Do you remember —

Q: — "children cry for Castoria— "

Nimitz: -- and I'm sure Father had bought his share of it for his kids, but that's about all!

Q: It was a patent medicine of sorts.

Nimitz: Yes. Dad probably thought of them as medicine men, being a Texan -- "no good Indian but a dead Indian."

Q: Mrs. Nimitz, won't you join us and give us some of your reflections on your father-in-law?

Joan Nimitz: I think I've said my all.

Q: You haven't said it on tape, though, you see. You were talking before dinner about the personal attributes of the man -- I mean, aside from his military nature, but the personal attributes of the man. Do you want to recall some of these things?

Joan Nimitz: Well, I think that he was so remarkably good in everything he did. It always was surprising to me that anybody as straightford and good and unselfish as he was could possibly have got as far as he did. You know? This is perhaps a little bit skeptical, but you always think of a person who succeeds as somebody who perhaps is looking out for himself.

Q: The man who elbows his way is the man who succeeds?

Joan Nimitz: Yes, and there wasn't any element of this that I could ever see, anywhere.

Nimitz: Nor any element of impatience. As I say, he was a very serene person.

Joan N.: And to think that as a 15 year old boy he went to the Naval Academy, from a very humble background. You feel that perhaps he would have had to be rather a pushy sort of a person to have made it. But he never was.

Q: But in his case was there not something else which stood him in good stead, his ability to see an objective and work for it with an unswerving --

Joan N.: Yes, he was very very persevering. But not a bulldozer type of persevering. There wasn't any pushing other people over as he went, ever. Of course, he really only thought about other people.

Nimitz: Something I've been thinking about -- what he was probably best at, aside from motivating people charismatically with this obvious seeing in them only the best -- what I think he did very very well, and that was value to any industry or anybody else, any other kind of endeavor that he took part in, is that he really understood, in some unique fashion, the intricacies of organization, in that he would organize and set policy in such a fashion that was so philosophically logical and correct that he then never got himself in a box. He would say, "What are the decisions I should make? What are the decisions the next echelon must perforce make? And the echelon beyond that? And what are the irreversible ones that the next echelon above must not make?" And he would organize along that fashion, and literally make the decision he had to make, and I'm sure he was perffectly content, perfectly able then to go to sleep, knowing that the inevitable result was that the best was going to come out of that organization, and he could do no more. I really think, everywhere he went, you'd find tha t therewas a relatively peaceful structure. The decision making and the authority and the responsibilities were so extraordinarily logically constructed, and the credit given, as far down as it could, all the way back, that it made it very easy to run the outfit.

Q: This compels some statement about his intellectual ability. Everything you say seems to indicate a superior kind of intellect which could plan and so forth. Do you want to talk about that?

Nimitz - 28

I mean, in terms of illustration, if you can?

Joan N.: I don't know that I would know how to put it. He was a terribly clear thinker.

Nimitz: He was a very clear thinker. Let me give you an example. Too bad a guy you can't talk to, I don't know whether you can or not, is Robert Sproul, who was president of University of California, when Dad went there to found the NROTC unit. Bob Sproul saw enough of Dad to put Dad on the faculty appointment committee, to choose professors for tenure and promotion, and if ever there was a political environment, it is a university campus, and particularly one as big and powerful as University of California. And Sproul did it because he recognized that Dad was a very clear thinker, and was able to separate the important from the unimportant in what a man had done in life. And incidentally, this ability to distinguish between the important and the trivial is part and parcel of this ability to organize and set goals and tasks, and then essentially stand back. I really think bums rose to the occasion.

Q: It indicates an intellect of different dimensions.

Joan N: A great faith in people, too, and tremendous interest in people. I mean, people really were Dad's whole life.

Nimitz: Yes. Just to give you an example, I'll bet you Dad was better than Jim Farley ever thought of being at remembering names.

Joan N: Yes.

Nimitz: And that's symptomatic of an interest in people. One day when Dad and Mother were living in Long Beach in an apartment, when Dad had command of Battleship Division One, I think it was -- the flagship was the Arizona -- and Joan and I were ensigns down in San Diego. We'd come up to visit them on a weeknd. We'd been swimming. It was fall and they were living in this apartment on the beach at Long Beach, and we'd come in. Everybody, Dad and Mother and Noan and I, sort of cold and chisley and dying for an old fashioned, which Dad had gone out in the kitchen to make, when the doorbell rang and an elderly gentleman -- he must have been 80 if he was a day -- appeared at the door and said, "Is this where Admiral Nimitz lives?"

We said, "Yes," all of us in wet bathing trunks and what not, and he said, "Well, I've come to call on him."

I wasn't old enough then to just nail him and say pointblank, "What's your name, old boy?"

He came in and he planked himself down, very taciturn, and my mother tried to engage him in coversation, with very little success. And finally Dad came in, and Dad took one ook at him, and it was perfectly apparent that Dad was terribly nonplussed.

and in a spot, so Dad said, "Will you have an old fashioned?" — so he could beetle back into the kitchen. And he did, he made a fifth old fashioned, and he came back in, and to all of our embarrassment, he handed this guy the old fashioned, and then instead of being his normal cordial self he just sort of stood there and stared at him. And finally, all of a sudden, the light shone in his eyes and he said, "I know who you are! You're old Crotchett," or whatever his name was. "You were a bos'n on the f'ks'le of the Panay when I was the skipper back in the Philippines in 1906."

And the old guy said, "Yes, yes, of course."

Joan N: Like "what's the matter with you?"

Nimitz: "Are you losing your marbles?"

Q: You spoke before about his humility, and this word has re-occurred several times also in your conversation, Mrs. Nimitz. I recall him talking about the Battle of Midway and about Admiral Spruance, saying that Admiral Spruance won the war in the Pacific.

Joan N: This would be very typical of him, I think.

Q: Is this not an illustration of humility?

Nimitz - 31

Nimitz: Yes, but I think it's a little more than that, in deference to Admiral Spruance. If you phrase it another way, Dad , "In your opinion, of the people who worked for you, who did most to contribute toward a/~~war~~ victory in the Pacific?" he would say "Admiral Spruance" every time. If you'd say, "You mean in a fighting capacity, a command at sea capacity?" he'd probably say, "Yes," and then if you said, "How about in a staff capacity?" he'd probably say, "Well. . ."

"You realize, when they came ashore, they planned, it would be tossup there between Admiral Spruance and Admiral Sherman." That was the way he'd put it, I'm sure.

Joan N: He often talked about the young aviator, do you remember-- Gay, was that his name?

Nimitz: Oh, yes.

Joan N: He loved to talk about that, and he was terribly fond of that young man.

Nimitz: Gay was the man who was --

Joan N: -- the only survivor ---

Nimitz: -- during the Battle of Midway, from hiding under neath his life raft, you remember?

Nimitz - 32

Q: Yes.

Joan N.: A young pilot. He was the only survivor of the whole squadron, I think.

Nimitz: Of that squadron.

Q: What did he say about him?

Joan N: He said what a wonderful guy he was and how remarkable it was, and he admired him tremendously, I think.

Nimitz: You know, Dad never saw a shot fired in anger, don't forget. I used to tell him time and again, "I know more about naval warfare than you'll know if you live to be a thousand." "I have participated in it, both in this war and the Korean War." And I just know that Dad was fascinated by the intrepid quality of aviators who fought sort of single handed -- and Marines, who also were pretty single handed about a lot of things. And you could see why, as the guy sitting back in the sanctuary directing operatins and, you know, hoping and praying they were going to be successful and so forth, you must have gotten this fantastic affection for these guys who were obviously cutting the mustard, particularly these younger guys who, you know, really weren't trained very long for that sort of thing.

Nimitz - 33

Q: But this doesn't mean that he played down in any way the role of the submariners.

Nimitz: Oh my God no!

Q: Talk about that.

Nimitz: Well, the way of putting it is, if you turned on the faucet Dad would talk about submarines.

Q: I knew he would. You do so also.

Nimitz: Well, I think it would be wrong to, in any way, shape or form, ever give the impression that Dad felt, you know, in a freshman like attitude toward submarines above all else. I am sure that he realized that what the submarines did, they did very well, and they were brave and resourceful and so on, but I don't think -- it would be a wrong concept to say that he felt that anything won the war other than the carrier task forces, in the long run. They did, that's all there was to it. The carrier task forces and the Marines.

Joan N: I was going to say, what about the Marines?

Nimitz: And the Marines.

Joan N: OK.

Nimitz: But the Marines could not have functioned without those carrier task forces. That's the point. And I think that's rather remarkable in a man who was not an aviator. He was offered the opportunity to go to Pensacola at the same time Ernie King was and several others, when the Navy realized they had to get some people in senior positions through Pensacola, to have an appreciation and a grasp. And when Joana L went to the keel laying of the carrier Nimitz, and at a luncheon afterwards, because they had to recognize that somebody was there named Nimitz, they asked me to say a few words, and the point I made was, "I think it's absolutely fitting that the carrier be named Nimitz, because really he did appreciate its employment very quickly, and I think as well as was required, which meant as well as any naval aviator would have appreciated its importance."

All of his major commanders commanded carrier task forces.

Joan N: Incidentally, I think that was a terribly good short speech that Chester made, and you ought to have a copy of it.

Nimitz: Oh, Ellis got a copy.

Joan N: Has he? That's right. He was there, wasn't he?

Q: Was he ever tempted to have training at Pensacola?

Nimitz: Oh, yes, you betcha.

Q: Did he try?

Nimitz: No, he didn't try, at all. The reason he didn't, he says to me and to his family, is because he felt he had a responsibility to a wife with young children growing up, and that he might get himself killed in an airplane. I always felt that rang rather hollow, in the light of the fact that he spent his time in submarines instead, and there wasn't a nickel's worth of choice between them, as far as the statistics of the situation were concerned. As it turned out, in wartime submarines lost a higher percentage by a considerable amount than aviators, of those employed, on a percentage basis.

Q: Well, there certainly was no encouragement for a young naval officer to go to Pensacola, on the part of senior officers of that time.

Nimitz: Well, I think there was. A senior officer -- I think really any senior officer who was ambitious should have seen the light. You were not going to be a big wheel in our Navy unless you either were very outstanding, or had flight training. Now, if you were both, you were bound to win, like King. But it made a lot of people like -- well, the man we were talking about before supper, and many others of his time, admirals when they never would have been by any other kind of measure. But we had to have people of that age group to direct operations in which you're expending young aviators, and as a young aviator I damned well would want an aviator involved -- even though it was lip service more than in fact good judgment. I'd say Sherman was a clearcut case of a guy who was outstanding, and had the perspicacity to go and take the training.

Q: Do you have any recollection of the way in which your father approached the high command that was coming his way at the time of Pearl Harbor? How he felt about it?

Nimitz: No, I don't, because I was --

Joan N: -- you were away.

Nimitz: I was away.

Joan N: I was there when Dad left Washington. I'd been there about a week. And I know the thing he did just before -- that very day that he left, was to go to Mary's school. I suppose Mary was about 11, was she, or 12, something like that -- to some performance that she was in. He and Mother went to that, and then Dad came back and had a sandwich and got on the train and went.

Q: And he went by train into California, didn't he?

Joan N.: Yes.

Q: He made this point, when I talked with him, and seemed to welcome this opportunity of a rather long trip across country --

Joan N: -- to collect himself --

Q: -- to get organized, to think, and he had a young --

Joan N: -- Lamar went with him.

Q: Yes, Lamar. Did he ever reflect on what he found at Pearl Harbor and his reactions?

Nimitz: Yes, I heard him once say how absolutely incredibly overpoweringly dismal it was. You know, imagine a guy -- you've got the picture of him now, completely dedicated to the US Navy, serene in his confidence, of everything about the US Navy, arriving on the scene and seeing the US Navy in a complete state of disarray and debacle. It really did take a person of his confidence to restore morale. No question about it, if he did nothing else, that was a smart decision. I've often wondered, and I really don't know, who was the smart cookie who put the finger on Dad for that spot. I've never really given that much thought, but that guy was a genius in understanding what was required in the situation.

Q: Was King perhaps involved in it?

Nimitz: He might have been. I really don't know. Dad had a great admiration for King, and understood King too very well. I never heard Dad say anything -- well, I never heard him say anything really bad about anybody -- but I did about Forrestal. He was disturbed by Forrestal. But he certainly never had anything but the highest praise for King. I'm sure he understood that King wasn't the most emotionally human guy in the world, but that's neither here nor there. That's not what King was paid for.

Joan N: I remember Dad saying that when he got to Pearl Harbor, that one of the overpowering things was the terrible smell of burning bodies. It just permeated the air. Absolutely nauseating and completely depressing, I'm sure. And this picture, was supposed to have been painted-- that was when he arrived at Pearl Harbor -- that was the background of the burning ships. Mother made the mistake one day of saying, "I hate that picture of Dad, it makes him look so cross, and I've never seen him with his hands in his pockets that way." And Chester said, "Well, if you don't like it, I do," and took it right off the wall, and that's how we got it.

(Three in no page 39)

Nimitz - 40

Q: Well, in spite of the devastating scene and the shock that it caused, it didn't really overturn his serenity, his confidence?

Joan N: No, I don't think anything ever really affected that. I think he always was able to bounce out of it, don't you? I've never seen him ---

Nimitz: --- well, because he always thought he was on the side of the right, I'm afraid.

Q: How does one arrive at this conviction? How did he arrive at his conviction that he was always on the side of the right?

Nimitz: Well, let's face it, in the first place, he happened to have been. You know, why rationalize what were the circumstances? And here was Dad, who had marched as a passed midshipman -- not as a midshipman, but as a young officer he'd marched at the funeral of Admiral Togo. He was a great admirer of the Japanese. There was an admiral who used to make the run down the so called Slot to Guadalcanal. I wish I could think of his name. Begins with an N -- that I thought was really one of the greatest naval officers that ever lived, when I read a brief synopsis of his life when he died, and Dad had sent me a copy of it and said, "Chester, there is a naval officer." You know, it's always baffled me how he could be so -- how you can be very effective fighting an enemy that you really admire very highly.

Jean N: He was very competitive though, I think.

Nimitz: Oh, he was competitive, no doubt about that.

Q: Did he have admiration for Admiral Namura, with whom he was associated in Washington?

Nimitz: I don't know. I don't know that Dad would ever have met Namura. When Dad was in Washington, he was in Bureau of Navigation, and I doubt that was a level that would be likely to meet the Jap ambassador.

You know, a propos of nothing, the only kind of critical thing I've heard him say about people, because it referred to a certain person, and I've heard him say it about two or three people -- it was always the same criticism, when he really finally got frustrated, was -- "Chester, the guy is stupid. And I can put up with a stupid person as long as they are of good will, but when he is stupid and obstinate, Chester, that is a dangerous character." And I know two people he referred to as that, very clearly, which is sort of symptomatic of what he didn't prize, and by inference you can --

Let me tell you how his faith in the Navy was. Another thing -- I've always sort of felt nostalgic, and that the good days are really gone forever, when I think of this -- when I see some sailor standing at an intersection here on Connecticut thruway, trying to get back from New York on a weekend to New London or something. I can remember Dad saying, when Mother was apparently urging him to give his daughters suitable instructions, what should they do if they get in any binds or anything, Dad saying, "Listen, the same thing applies to all the children and to you yourself, dearest -- if ever you find you're in trouble" -- this was long before World War II -- " no matter where you are, if you see a bluejacket, call for him and tell him who you are, and you're in good hands."

This is how closeknit the Navy was. And Dad I'm sure knew half the sailors in the Navy at that time by name. Or with a little jogging, could.

Joan N: I thought you were going to talk about the days when he went out to China as a young past midshipman or whatever they called them. Do you remember?

Q: That was his first cruise out there, with a lot of his classmates.

Nimitz: Then when he got promoted to ensign, he then got command of what was called in those days a destroyer. It was just simply a fantastic life. I can see how he grew up with this fantastic affection for the Navy, that nobody in my time could have possibly grown up with. If anybody did, it's Hal Bowen. I don't know how he did it.

Q: Your father told me about one man whom he was forced to dismiss from his command, and his technique apparently in dealing with this man, whom he liked as a person, was that he turned it in on the man and made him admit his inadequacies.

Nimitz: Yes, Ghormley, I think.

Q: Yes. Was this a customary technique?

Nimitz: I don't know. I don't really know. I certainly know of that case, and I do know that the Navy Department was apparently completely conscienceless about sending flag officers who were white elephants, and for whom they couldn't find a reasonable assignment, out to the staff of CINCPAC, with the pretty well founded conviction that Dad would make use of them in some manner that was worthwhile. You know, I'm sure that Dad understood this business of face saving, and preserve their self respect and so forth, —

Joan N: Well, I think one of the remarkable things — I don't know whether you mentioned it — was that when he got out to

Nimitz - 44

Pearl Harbor, the very first thing he did was not to change anybody on that staff. They just all stayed and he was delighted to have them. Which I think very few people would have done.

Nimitz: Well, I think that was a great insight. That's astute.

Joan N.: Yes, but most people would have come with their own team.

Nimitz: Oh, he always warned me, never ask for anybody and never develop your own team, because it absolutely destroys your flexibility and free-handedness. If you are dissatisfied with the material that is ordered to you by the Navy Department, you have no previous ties, you're not beholden, and you simply say, "Young man" or whoever it is "you are not cutting the mustard, and I herewith dispense with you." And I agree that's very sound advice. So many people, both in the military and in politics, I think, make the mistake of continuing to drag in their old cronies who ultimately --

Joan N: -- then they can't get rid of them --

Nimitz: -- get to be real liabilities.

Q: You said several times, you talked about his concern, his awareness of other people, and I wondered if this awareness expressed itself in compassionate terms sometimes? I'm thinking especially of Admiral Kimmel.

Nimitz: Oh, yes. Dad would be the first one to say, "There but for the grace of God go I, and why not? Because I wasn't in the job." You know. Anybody in the Navy who doesn't think that is also crazy, because that is the circumstance. All you have to do is read any of the background. It is a circumstance.

Q: Did he express this in terms of personal friendship for the man?

Nimitz: Oh yes, you betcha. He invited Admiral Kimmel out to Pearl and I think Admiral Kimmel came, once or twice, during the war, to come and visit the headquarters and stay there. Oh, he was very much --

Joan N: Well, he was a terribly generous person.

Nimitz: You know Admiral MacDonald, that great old --

Joan N: -- yes, who lived in Oakland --

Nimitz: -- who lived in San Jose, I think.

Joan N: And I think Dad was terribly good and very fond and loyal to Bruce

Kanaga, don't you think?

Nimitz: Yes, a classmate. The people he knew well or saw frequently enough, he had great admiration for. It's very strange. I'll tell you another man for whom Dad had an extraordinary admiration, and that was President Truman.

Joan N: Yes.

Nimitz: Dad was enough of a student of human nature to see that there was almost the epitome of the American concept, of his concept of Americans. Take a man of good will, no matter how humble a background, and thrust him into the position, and if he's a man of good will and you demonstrate your confidence, as you had to when you elected him, he will rise to the occasion. You know, this is the "American Dream." And I think it worked pretty well.

Q: This was not the attitude of the sophisticated Easterner.

Joan N: No, no, never. Really, very unsophisticated, except for this really natural dignity that is sophistication --

Nimitz: -- yea, I think that business is that the unsophisticated Texan is a far better politician and is a better predictor of what was going to happen, and he sees a little bit more unbeclouded by these sophistications.

Q: You mean there's no veneer there.

Nimitz: You're damned right. Well, but they'd also not demand any credit by a bunch of false values. I think that the Midwest and Texas thought Truman would win and never had any doubt about it. Nobody in the East ever could dream of Truman winning, because they'd just lost touch, with the general public.

Q: Talk about this personal dignity which he possessed to such a degree.

Joan N: Well, I think it was absolutely sort of a graciousness of manner which may be sophisticated people have by acquiring it, but I'm sure Dad was born with it. He really didn't have to think about it. He just didn't make a wrong move of any sort. He never did anything gauche, I don't think.

Nimitz: No. That's a good point.

Joan N: Even though he came from this very humble background, and none of it was ever put on or learned anywhere. You felt it was just part and parcel of the way he behaved, whether it was the accepted pattern or not. And it always was perfectly charming.

I mean, people just adored it the whole way. And none of it was corny. I don't think Dad was corny. Did you feel that way?

Q: No, indeed not.

Joan N: I think he was sentimental about a great many things.

Q: That graciousness toward a total stranger ---

Joan N: I think he was sentimental about many things. I think he was sentimental about your mother, tremendously so.

Nimitz: That's what I said, I thought he was sentimental about Mother, but not about the rest of his children.

Joan N: Well, I think he was very family minded. He ceertainly was sentimental about his grandchildren.

Nimitz: I say, after he retired he became far more so.

Joan N: Yes.

Q: We talked a little about in retirement, about a more detached attitude toward this sense of duty that was so all-pervasive.

Nimitz - 49

Joan N: Yes. I remember that when he retired, I'm sure that Chester's mother hoped that he would do something to occupy himself. Here he was, just full of energy and ability and good mind and everything else, and here he was just going to sit, because he wouldn't take a job of any sort. Totally disinterested in finances or money. He never handled any of the money in the family, you know. Mother did all of that. And he didn't care about money at all, so he didn't want a job for money, and he didn't feel that he could take a sort of a commercial type of job. The only thing he did was that United ZNations job.

Q: Yes, tell me about that, Kashmire, the plebiscite.

Joan N: I think he was delighted to do that, and I think it was too bad really that the UN didn't use him in some other capacity.

Q: From all the things you say about him he was eminently suited for a diplomatic assignment.

Joan N: And I really think it was a tragedy that it wasn't UN. I think Dad would have done a darned good job with anything there, and I think he would havebeen very happy doing it. But as it was, he just really sort of vegetated. He said once, "Well, now, Mother is the one. I've spent all my life doing things because the Navy wanted me to. Now I'm retired. She is the one who is going to decide where we live and what we do."

Q: He did have some decided interests, however, in his old age, did he not? Wasn't he passionately interested in the subject of oceanography?

Nimitz: I wouldn't say passionately, no.

Joan N: He was a great reader. He read all the time, and I'm sure he had a lot of interests. I think he was very interested in making fresh water out of salt water in California. I remember him talking at great length about that. But I mean, I don't think he was very involved in it anyway. And of course he was a trustee at the University-- I mean a regent.

Q: Didn't he have some active concern also in the preservation of historical monuments and things like that in California?

Nimitz: Oh, I think only incidental to having stubled across some walking around the Bay. He was a great walker. I don't --

Q: -- he talked about that with great--

Joan N: -- yes, he was interested, yes he was, he was interested in that sort of thing.

Nimitz - 51

Nimitz: But that had never been an avocation or interest before, before they lived in the area and walked around there.

Joan N: But then Dad didn't really have any hobbies. I can't think of a single hobby. He loved to play tennis when he was younger, you know. But -- he really didn't have hobbies. I think this was one of the pathetic things, really.

Q: How closely did he keep in touch with his peers, in his latter years?

Joan N: When he was at Yerba Buena he must have seen quite a lot of Navy people.

Nimitz: But I don't think that there was any deliberate attempt to keep himself informed about what was going on in the Navy. The Secretary of the Navy would ask him occasionally to come back and serve on plucking boards and that kind of thing. But I think he understood instinctively that "the king is dead, long live the king" concept in the Navy was an essential one, and as I say, he was a little bit disturbed about the general downplaying of the influence of the professional officer, as the Pentagon civilian superstructure proliferated.

Q: I had the feeling, I don't know why, when he was at Yerba

Nimitz - 52

Buena, that it was like dwelling on Olympus, and all the lesser naval figures were pretty much removed from him there.

Nimitz: Oh, I think so. He had no part and parcel of them.

Joan N: Oh, people were in and out of that house all the time, visiting him.

Nimitz: Just socially, not —

Joan N: Yes. Yes, and this he loved. I mean, you know, the house could be filled with people all the time and Dad would be perfectly happy. Particularly Navy people. Particularly young Navy people.

Q: Before World War II, how often did the family move somewhere near to his tour of duty? Was there a great deal of this?

Joan N: You always went.

Nimitz: Yes, except for — now, when I was four and five years old, he went off on a cruise to Australia, and we lived in Brooklyn for about eight months he was gone, but other than that, we lived at his port or base always. San Pedro a good deal. The War Collge at Newport, Norfolk, Honolulu, Berkeley, San Diego —

we were generally at the base. We were generally in the vicinity. I'd say the children were away more at school and what not than the question of his being absent.

Q: As you reflect on his career, what command, what assignment proved to be for him the most rewarding, the one that he really liked best?

Nimitz: Well, my guess is, whether he was consciously aware of it or not, but it would be just a guess, was that the assignments that were most important toward fitting him for the job of a full admiral, whether in the Pacific or Washington, were the assistant chief of staff on the staff of CINCFLEET ? back in 1924, or something like that, and ---

Joan N: Admiral Robinson?

Nimitz: -- Admiral Robinson, and the assistant chief of Bureau of Navigation and the chief of Bureau of Navigation. The rest of the jobs, his submarine duties and so forth, were simply, as far as I'm concerned, familiarization with the mechanics of the sea going Navy, but they don't tend to fit you for higher command. You don't see much of the broad picture, as you do on the CINC staff and in Bureau of Navigation trying to man the Navy. So as far as those in which he learned most, and in which the evaluation of his superior was probably most critical to his subsequent success, I'd say those were the jobs.

Joan N: There were two jobs that he had which I would say indicated his ability to get along with nothing, the way he had to when he got to Pearl Harbor, a sort of challenge of, "I can still do it, by George," and one was building the submarine base at Pearl Harbor, which he did from nothing. You know, he had to send scouts out at night to steal material --

Q: -- I'm glad you mentioned that --

Joan N: -- to get the place going. And the other one was really starting the NROTC in Berkeley, which he did from nothing.

Q: Was that the first unit that set up, at Berkeley? Was that the prototype?

Nimitz: Well, you see, both of these required -- there were seven of them established simultaneously. Berkeley was one of them. This ability to scrounge and get along with nothing he never lost, in his complete lack of conscience about stealing fruit if he could reach it over the fence.

Joan N: Yes, this good honest man I've been talking about -- isn't that funny?

Nimitz - 55

Nimitz: He used to carry a cane. He used to carry a hooked cane, so he could pull the branches toward him. That must have been a Texas tradition.

Q: This is a kind of casuistry. A number of them men with whom I've talked have made it perfectly clear, to use President Nixon's expression, that their eye was always on the thing that would lead them to command, that they were born to command and this was the objective, and anything that was a deviation, they really didn't care too much for. Right?

Nimitz: Yes, I'd say that was him.

Joan N: Yes, I think he was fairly astute at that.

Nimitz: You're damned right.

Joan N: Taking the sort of job, or asking for the sort of job that he felt would be the best for his career. But then there always seems to be (crosstalk) looking out for you in that way, don't you think, if they spot you as good?

Nimitz: Yes, I think so.

Q: Probably more so in the Navy as he knew it and grew up in it.

Nimitz   Rivht.

Q: It's so diversified.

Joan N: But I've known of Chester having duty pressed on him because it was good for his career, when we would have preferred it differently.

Q: Don't stay too long in one spot. One other event. Admiral Nimitz spoke about the submarine base, and spoke with some feeling about that accomplishment. One other thing that he talked about with obvious relish, in his early career, was that assignment in Germany on the diesel engines. He felt this was very significant.

Nimitz: Well, of course, it was significant for one thing in that it gave him and mother a free honeymoon abroad.

Joan N: Which your mother didn't enjoy.

Nimitz: Well, I don't know whether she did or not.

Joan: I always had very dubious --

Nimitz: -- but it was certainly a feather in his cap, as being

-- as recognition of a sufficient engineering understanding and know-how to be sent abroad to bring back this new technology to the United States Navy, and see if we couldn't build one of them thar diesel engines. And then he was the -- I don't really know in what capacity -- he was supervising the installation of diesel engines in the Maumee when he lost a finger, pointing to a couple of gear wheels going this way. I told him, in my day at the Naval Academy they told us to keep our fingers out of the gears!

Joan N: What saved his whole hand from going in was his Naval Academy ring. It was that finger.

Q: Oh, that would have been detrimental to his career.

Joan N: Yes. He had a lot of fun with that missing finger, though; it was one of his stock games with young children, was to pull and pull and pull and pull his finger right off, and then show this stump, you know.

Nimitz: And then put it back on, pull the other hand.

Joan N: All kinds of tricks.

Q: Charming.

Nimitz - 58

Joan N: He was great for tricks. He loved card tricks. And of course he was, as you know, a great collector of jokes. On the Arizona they had a club you could belong to if you could tell the admiral a joke he hadn't heard. Real collection of them. And Betsey, our middle daughter, visited with them, oh, I'd say perhaps two summers before Dad died, and they were in Yerba Buena. She took a course at Berkeley that summer, and she said, "You know, Mother, Grandpa is wonderful with his tales at dinner parties, but I've found out how he does it. He has them all written down in a little book, at least the punch lines, and he doesn't get them wrong." This is, you know, after he was 80.

Q: This was a concession to age.

Nimitz: Yes, like the Old Man who started to write the quotations on his cuff.

Joan N: "He leaves the dinner party and goes into the bathroom and bones up on his stories, and comes back and tells them, so they're fresh in his mind and he doesn't make a mistake."

Q: So he had a certain amount of pride in his reputation which he was going to maintain.

Joan N: Yes. Oh, yes.

Nimitz: That's part and parcel of his whole post-retirement. He was maintaining an image until he died.

Joan N: For the Navy.

Nimitz: For the Navy.

Q: And this is another application of the sense of duty.

Nimitz: Yes. Yes. Whether it was misplaced or not, I don't know, but in any case that certainly was the reason. Supposing he'd stayed with the United Nations. I question which is the greater. I don't know.

Joan N: I think he would have been very happy to have done that, frankly. But he wasn't going to go and ---

Nimitz: --- he left the United Nations himself because he felt that they were trying to keep this Kashmir k Plebiscite Commission organized and intact long after there was any hope of India ever allowing it to function, and he felt it was conscienceless for people to sit there and draw pay for a purpose that essentially had gone by the board irrevocably.

Q: Then, thinking in terms of the diplomatic maneuvering that our

Nimitz - 60

people have to engage in with the Russians, he probably wouldn't have been able to do that, would he? I mean, the interminable conferences where nothing happens.

Nimitz: Oh, I think he would.

Joan N: I think he would. He was terribly patient.

Nimitz: He was patient, yes.

Joan N: And dogged.

Nimitz: He was patient, and furthermore, you know, I'm sure he would have thought to himself, by God, I'll make an impression on them because I am going to ultimately make them my friends, and the instant they become my friends they are going to be less able as opponents. He was almost Oriental in his -- I guess it's a Southern outlook, but by gosh, he was plenty patient, and could play that waiting game with a grand smile and all that goes with it.

Joan N: He might get just that sharp glint in his eyes, I'll tell you sometimes he was really steely-eyed. You didn't see it very often, but --

Nimitz: -- that always gave you an insight into the probability of --

Joan: Oh brother, did that get a cold look!

Nimitz: When you saw it normally was when Dad had somehow had it forced upon his attention that some organization or individual was not in fact of good will, and he now had proof of it.

Q: The conviction had arrived at that moment.

Tell me about the admiral's fabulous memory.

Joan N: Well, even when he was an oldman of 80, he would sit in a room and start telling a story of some sort, and sometimes a rather long, involved, slowly delivered story with a punch line later on, and you sat and listened for a while, and maybe if you were the cook, like me, you'd have to run to the kitchen --

Nimitz: -- oh, and he'd say, "Now, dearest, what was that man's name?" And mother would come up with a few names and he'd say, "No, Sphinx, pinkx -- Smith, that was it, Smith," and by golly, it would be right in the dark ages.

Joan N: I would go back in the kitchen, stir my stew, put on my water or something, come back five minutes later. He would have stopped the story because he didn't want me to miss t, and as I'd walk into the room, he would pick up right where he'd left off, even though there'd been an intervening conversation, and he'd go on methodically.

Q: Even though there'd been this, and he'd been part of this, intervening conversation.

Joan: Oh yes, and he would pick up right where he'd left off with the story and carry it right through without a bumble anywhere. Quite incredible ability to do that, keep on the track.

Nimitz: Yes, but I think this is associated so much with his interest in people.

Joan N: Yes. Oh yes.

Q: This is probably the thing that kept him alive mentally.

Joan N: And the Navy was his love all right, but the Navy was people.

Nimitz: Well, we were saying that his memory stemmed from his interest in people, and Joan made the point that he really wasn't interested in the guns and technology of the Navyk. And I think that it is that aspect that made him rationalize in his own mind my getting out of the Navy. I think he sensed that the Navy had ceased to become a Navy of people, and had become a technological machine, and I think it's borne out today -- the powerful men in the Navy, whether the straight line officers know it or not, are not in the line at all. They are in the procurement cycle in this military industrial complex, spending billions of dollars on the technology of the Navy, and it is the perhaps less intellectually able type that is left in the so called direct line. I don't -- I'm sure that's the opinion of the civilian hierarchy that runs the Navy and the procurement. They're far more interested in where the dollars go than the specific ability or intellect of the leaders per se. I think they discount the necessity for inspirational leadership any more anyway, and there may be a lot in that too, you know. How inspirational, of what import is inspirational leadership in combating a Polaris missile that's falling vertically out of the sky with a nuclear warhead?

Joan N: I think we'd have less anti-Vietnam riots, though, perhaps, if we had a little more leadership.

Nimitz: But the fact is, Dad was a people man entirely. Bureau of Navigation -- Dad never heard of the Bureau of Ordnance, I'm sure, except he sent one of my directors named Paul Hammond back during the war to say, "Get the Bureau of Ordnance straightened out." Dad told me, "You know, I knew I had done it when he'd been back there 48 hours and I got a message from Blandy, I guess it was, saying 'Get this guy out of here.' "

Q: You know, so many things you've said about Admiral Nimitz have put me in mind of General Eisenhower, the personal aspect, the warmth, the compassion all of this.

Joan: right.

Nimitz: Yes, and you know, I'm quite confident that the essence -- that's why I'd really like to sort of see you get finished with talking to my Mother and my family and me -- the essence is to nail these contemporary associates of his down before they die, because that's where the real meat of his naval business, in a manner I could never tell you, will come to pass. For instance, I don't know what Spruance --

Joan N: Spruance is in a very bad way, I've heard.

Nimitz: Yes, but you see, it's just terrible for Spruance to -- Spruance knows more about my father than any of us will ever know, and the same, people like Harry Hill, General Kelly Turner, some of the Marines, those are the guys.

Joan N: There must have been people on his staff, dear, that we don't know or don't think of.

?/?(crosstalk)
Nimitz: Jean Plucky would be -- (Adm. Jean Fluckey)
@ Fluckey

Q: I have a list of his staff members and I want to show it to you and have you indicate which ones you think would be of particular interest.

Nimitz: He never discussed his staff with me. I really wouldn't know.

I'd say that any one of them would be just as good as another, if the guy's alive and has his mind.

Joan N: Depending, I was going to say, on their intelligence also. (crosstalk)

Nimitz: -- . . . at that level if he wasn't . . . .

Q: Is Lamar available anywhere?

Nimitz: Yes, he is , and I'll tell you who knows how to get in touch with him is Judge Eller.

Q: Because your father himself mentioned Lamar as someone with him he had, at points, in Honolulu -- (crosstalk)

Nimitz: -- . . .know a lot about him, that's all there is to it. Lamar has to know a lot about him. And Lamar's an intellectually smart potato, don't worry. Mercer was another one.

Q: Admiral Mercer.

Joan N: Yes, Mercer, and Tommy Thompson. I think Tommy Thompson died, didn't he? I thought he was on the staff.

INDEX

for

INTERVIEW

with

Rear Admiral Chester W. Nimitz, Jr., USN (Ret.)

Anderson, Admiral Walter, 24

Aquinas, Sister Mary (Nimitz), 16

Bowen, Hal, 43

Eisenhower, General Dwight D., 63

Forrestal, James, 13-14, 38

Gay, Ensign George H., 31

Halsey, Admiral William Frederick, 11-12

Hammond, Paul, 63

Kanage, Bruce, 45-46

Kimmel, Admiral Husband Edward, 45

King, Admiral Ernie J., 34-35, 38

Lamar, Captain Howell A., USNR (Ret.), 38

MacDonald, Admiral David L., USN (Ret.), 45

Montgomery, General Bernard Law, 2

Naval Academy, 19-20

Nimitz, Mary (see Aquinas)

Nomura, Admiral Kichisaburo, Imperial Japanese Navy, (Ret.), 41

Robinson, Admiral S. S., 23, 53

Sherman, Admiral Forrest, 14, 31

Sproul, Robert, 28

Spruance, Admiral Raymond Ames, 12, 30-31

Truman, President Harry, 14, 46

Vinson, The Honorable Carl, 17

Interview with Captain James T. Lay and Catherine Nimitz Lay

Subject: Fleet Admiral Chester A. Nimitz

Place: Newport, Rhode Island

Date: Monday evening, 16 February 1970

Capt. L.: You'll want to talk to Catherine. She knows most of the history of the family.

Q: Well, I suppose so, Sir. But you knew the Admiral in a different capacity at first. Would you tell me about your first meeting with him? I assume it was when you went as a young ensign to the Augusta, was it?

Capt. L.: I was ordered to the Augusta just before they sailed to China. I was on board the Portland before that, and I'd been away from home about a year and I wanted to get home. So I came home on leave to Missouri from the West Coast, from Bremerton, Washington, and I had gotten back just the day before the Augusta sailed.

Q: What year was this?

Capt. L.: This was in 1933 - in October '33. And I moved my stuff across the dock from the Portland to the Augusta and moved aboard at night. We sailed the next morning. Of course, being new on board, I didn't have any job assigned, so they said, "Well, come up on the bridge and see how we get under way."

Q: A lot of your classmates were on board...

Capt. L.: They were on board, yes, already...

Q: This looked like a delightful prospect for you, I should imagine.

Capt. L.: Right. And I had been requesting China duty, you know, on my fitness reports and so forth. In fact, on the Portland I used to go by the Executive Officer's office where there was a chief yeoman and I'd say, "When are my orders to China coming in?" And he said, "Oh, they'll be in shortly," and surprisingly they did come in by dispatch, and so I had about 20 days after having got en my orders until I joined the Augusta. Then when we sailed, well, having no assigned duties, Captain Nimitz said, well, I could be assistant navigator. So I had the pleasure of being on the bridge practically the whole time, all the way to...

Q: Had you had any experience in navigation?

Capt. L.: Well, I had won the sextant at the Naval Academy for standing One in the class on navigation.

Q: Oh, I see.

Capt. L.: So it was a good chance to do my little practice in navigation.

Q: He knew this, of course?

Capt. L.: He knew this, yes. So I got to be on the bridge, you know, the entire way across, which took I think 20 or 21 days to go across in those days, and so I got to meet him on the bridge, and actually, well, after we got under way and got clear of the channel, I went in to make my official call, which every officer does, having to be introduced to the captain and call on him and I saw him daily from then on...

Q: How did he act on this official call? What was your impression of him?

Capt. L.: He was very interested in junior officers. He always was, and he always associated with them and took part in things, and this was when he was in China, he used to play tennis with the tennis teams, you see. And if we had a cribbage tournament, we used to always include him in. And he'd always take part in any activities going on like that, and I think he enjoyed being with the younger officers and meeting them, which is always a wonderful thing for any senior officer...

Q: Did he apparently have in mind their training? They were in a formative stage, and he was trying to mold them?

Capt. L.: Yes. Because he used to take pains to let us handle his ship. And I know one thing he used to do. He used to put a box over the side and then we'd maneuver around, each junior officer would have a chance to bring the ship up alongside the box like it was a dock. And this ship-handling experience came in very handy later on.

Q: Was he very critical if you didn't succeed in the objective?

Capt. L.: No. He never raised his voice and he'd say, "Well, if I was doing it, I would have done it this way," and you got the message right away that he was telling you how it was to be done, but then he didn't appear to be critical. But if you listened, why, you got the message very clear that this was experience talking. And going in and out of port, he'd let the junior officers handle the ship.

Q: That was an act of faith, wasn't it?

Capt. L.: It really was. Actually, it's harder to let somebody else handle your ship than it is to do it yourself. I found this out later on when I had command of a destroyer and also a cruiser, that it's very hard to, you know, sit back and watch somebody else, because you have to let them go to the limit, to let them decide when to start backing down or whatever they're supposed to do to keep from hitting the dock, but still if you jump in too quickly they don't learn, and if you wait too long you're apt to be in trouble. So...

Q: And you're always responsible?

Capt. L.: You're always responsible. And - well even later on when I had my destroyer, I found this was good training to me to handle a ship. I remember the first time I brought a destroyer in to San Diego, after I'd learned to handle a ship myself, and had an ensign as officer of the deck, and he was standing on one foot and then the other, and he turned round and said, "Captain, are you going to take the con?" and I said, no. And he says, "Well, what do you want me to do?" I said, "I want you to tie the ship up to that buoy." He says, "You mean ME?" And this was almost unheard of, but you have to let them do it, and before we got through we had some good ship-handlers.

Q: You were passing on a Nimitz lesson?

Capt. L.: Absolutely. A lesson I learned from Admiral Nimitz. He used to let us handle the ship and I remember one night it was dark and we were getting under way in Manila Bay and I had the deck, and he says, "Take her out," through the breakwater and all this. And I thought this was really something to be able to take a cruiser and go out with the captain standing there...

Q: The flagship!

Capt. L.: The flagship, yes. And he would trust me to do it. Of course, it was comforting to know that you had a nice experienced gentleman standing there watching you in case you got in trouble, but still, it was the way you learned, and you had to give the right orders to the rudder to make the right turn at the right time and the right speeds and all this. But he was a good teacher. And many times he used to stop in the middle of the ocean and throw a box over and call the officers up, one by one, even the engineering officers and have them maneuver the ship around - take the ship and make a turn around and come back and come alongside this box - just to get the feel of the ship.

Q: From your knowledge of the fleet, was this an unusual thing for an officer to do?

Capt. L.: Yes, yes. Because even later on I was surprised at the number of junior officers who had never handled a ship. And - well, to digress a little bit - when I had my destroyer, it was considered a drill if someone other than the captain handled the ship, and one quarter we were out in Japan and I used to have them log all these things, these drills, when someone other than the captain handled the ship, and I got a letter from the Commander, Destroyer Force, Pacific Fleet, saying that he had noted my last quarterly report, that the ship had gotten under way and come to anchor 121 times during the quarter. Paragraph 2, he had noticed that 91 times during the quarter, that someone other than the captain had handled the ship. Paragraph 3, we do not think the commanding officer is getting enough ship-handling experience. And the training command had this framed, because they said, what are we trying to do. This is exactly what we were trying to do - train the junior officers to handle a ship.

Q: Presumably, the captain already has the...

Capt. L.: Right, and it's harder to let someone else handle the ship than it is to do it yourself.

Q: I can understand that, certainly. What are some of your recollections of Admiral Nimitz - Captain Nimitz, then - on that cruise?

Capt. L.: Well, I guess it's really hard to pinpoint any particular thing...

Q: Yes, well, tell me about some of the - the Augusta made some diplomatic calls in various ports, didn't she?

Capt. L.: Right, and well, we'd go to Japan, for instance, and I remember one time when we were in, I guess it was Kobe, and each Japanese official came out and he used the same boat and we had about 8 or 9 calls one morning, and I had the deck. Each of them came in a big, tall silk hat, all dressed alike, and you couldn't really tell one from the other. And so we had formalities with the guard of the day to full guard and band, and we had a Lieutenant Pierce [Pearce (Edw. L.)] on board who was a Japanese-language student and he knew some of these people by sight. He figured he knew most of them. So he came out to assist me. He looked at them when they got out of the boat, they'd come up from down below in the boat - it was one of these little steamers - and as they got on the bottom of the gangway, he would say who it was. And you had to be prepared with full guard and band, and then you just had to pull off the band or something, you know, to give the lesser ones...

Q: The proper rank, yes.

Capt. L.: And I remember one of them came aboard and I had kind of ducked the band but I didn't have a chance to bring the guard, full guard, down to the guard of the day. So he got the full guard. Well, when he left, he got the full guard. And after he left, I told the captain well, I'd made an error,

I didn't have time to get rid of the full guard, so I gave him the same when he left as when he came aboard. He said, "That's right. Don't change it."

Q: He turned out to be of lesser rank, huh?

Capt. L.: Yes, he should have had just the guard of the day, which is one squad, see, instead of the full...but he got the full works, but the Admiral said, "Well, no, don't change it. If you make a mistake when he comes aboard, make the same mistake when he leaves."

Q: Live through it.

Capt. L.: Yes. So the fellow didn't really realize that there was a change, see, because there was no change because he thought this was the guard of the day. But I thought that was a fine philosophy that if you make one error when the gentleman comes aboard, well, don't change it later. Let him assume this was the way we do things when he leaves.

Q: It was on that cruise - and to Japan again - that you went for the funeral of Admiral Togo, wasn't it?

Capt. L.: Right.

Q: Tell me about that.

Capt. L.: Well, we had been ordered to be the U.S. representatives over there, and actually I didn't get to the funeral myself, but we did have troops march in the parade, and we were actually the official representatives and we had to do all the - you know, all the courtesies and so on, and make him a visit.

Q: What role did Captain Nimitz play? Do you know?

Capt. L.: Well, we had the Commander-in-Chief, Asiatic Fleet, aboard, who was a four-star admiral.

Q: That was Admiral Upham?

Capt. L.: Admiral Upham, that's he. So the captain and the admiral, of course, they went along as the official representatives, and the only thing the juniors had were the ones that marched in the parade - these were just lieutenant commanders and so forth. But I didn't personally get into that.

Q: You told me earlier that's where you met your wife.

Capt. L.: Well, after we left Yokohama and went around to Kobe, then Catherine had finished the University of California and came out on - I guess it was one of the President liners, and came in to Kobe, and she joined the family there, because Mrs. Nimitz was in Kobe at the time, and as we were getting ready to leave Kobe we had a reception on board for all the people who had entertained us, and Catherine was at the reception, having just arrived. That's where I met her for the first time.

Q: Was that a ticklish business - to be interested in the Captain's daughter?

Capt. L.: Well, then we went on up to Tsingtao, you know, and it was interesting, you know, because when the Captain and Mrs. Nimitz came out for dinner, well, Catherine may be with us in the wardroom, and when he'd leave the ship, you know, he'd send the gig back and say, "Let Ensign Lay use the gig when he wants to ~~to~~ take Catherine back ashore." So that was interesting, from that point of view.

Q: How did your shipmates react to this?

Capt. L.: Well, of course, she was in the same group with all the rest of us, so they all - there was an extra boat to ride, everybody after dinner we'd after   actually, would go ashore and do the night spots and what not, so this was normal procedure, I would say.

Q: The Nimitz family moved around quite a bit - Japan to China and the Philippines...

Capt. L.: They did not go to the Philippines. They stayed in Japan, I think, when the ship was down in the Philippines. I don't believe Catherine's ever been in the Philippines, but in Japan and Shanghai and Tsingtao ~~is~~ where we spent the summer.

Q: Did the Captain and his wife entertain the young officers from the Augusta very much?

Capt. L.: Well, we always had these official functions. We'd always have, you know, different functions ashore where we'd meet everybody. At the French Club, you see, we'd have a big ship's party and things like this, you see. And, of course, we'd be out to the house for dinner and things like this. He used to make it a point to invite various junior officers out from time to time. He was very good about it - always being sure that the junior officers got invited round. Of course, we did a lot of calling and things like that in those days, too, you know, which they don't do any more, really.

Q: You mean you called on senior officers?

Capt. L.: Oh, yes we went to call on all - you called on your own head of department and all the senior officers on the ship, the captain, the executive officer. This was expected of everyone to do this, you see. So you'd spend your Sunday afternoon going round calling and, of course, if you were married and lived ashore, then they'd return the calls, but for the bachelors on board, well, of course they didn't get to return the calls. They'd invite you out to dinner or something like this, you see. And we had frequent ship's parties, you know, at Tsingtao and at the French Club in Shanghai and so forth.

Q: The Nimitzes were awfully good hosts, weren't they?

Capt. L.: Very. Very good. Always made everybody feel perfectly at home and like they were always glad to see you, and even after they came back to Washington, I stopped in in Washington and just stopped in to pay my respects, you know, and, "Oh, come on out to the house for dinner." I went out to dinner that night.

Q: Did you go on that Australian trip?

Capt. L.: Yes.

Q: Cruise?

Capt. L.: Sydney and Melbourne and round to Fremantle.

Q: Are there any special recollections of that?

Capt. L.: I remember it was a wonderful cruise because - well, one thing when we got to Melbourne - we were there two weeks if I remember rightly - and everybody wanted to entertain you, and we had a big American society there, and I remember they told the Americans that they could have the last night in port. The rest of the time we were down there to visit Australians - we were going to see the Australians. And in Sydney, and Melbourne, too, well, you get so many invitations that they just sort of prorate them. Somebody will have to go to this party, and this one, and this one, and you have some place to go for lunch, some place else to the horse races in the afternoon, and some place else for cocktails, and some place else for dinner, and always end up at a big ball or something. The main recollection was that after a few days of this, it was quite tiring and people used to say, "Gee, I wish I had the duty today," because you were on eight hours' duty and you could sleep the other sixteen. Because you went to one of these balls at night and you got back in the morning about 4 to 6 o'clock in the morning, and you'd have quarters at eight, and at 10 o'clock you were off again. So sleep wasn't very plentiful in those days.

Q: What about the poor captain? He had to attend, didn't he?

Capt. L.: He had to attend a lot of these, and I'm sure he was just as tired as we were. He probably got in at a little bit more reasonable hour than the young boys, you know. But it was a really nice cruise.

Q: Yes, without any major problems or anything of this sort. After that cruise, what were your connections with the Nimitzes, I mean after that, especially with the captain, the Admiral?

Capt. L.: Well, see, he was in command I guess roughly about a year - 18 months, something like that - a year and a half, and he came on back to the States and Admiral Gygax relieved him. That's the picture you saw here, when he was being relieved by Admiral Gygax.

Q: Tell me about him giving over the command, I mean, and the plans made by the junior officers.

Capt. L.: Well, we were all dressed in our fore-and-aft hats, and you see in the pictures that we're dressed up for the change-of-command ceremony and he was going to leave immediately afterwards, and so we said it would be nice if we formed a boat crew - he was going to leave on either the President Line or the Dollar Line, I forget just which they called it in those days - a few berths up the river from where we were moored between buoys, so we said we would row him over, so they were around collecting up the crew, and I think I ended up being stroke - that's what it looks to me like here - stroke of the crew. Just as we were pulling away from the ship, Admiral Gygax [Geigax] came out and he had an old hat of the Admiral's, you see, and he threw it down and said, "Take everything with you," like he was sweeping clear...

Q: Yes.

Capt. L.: ...of the previous commanding officer. Then when we came back, we took this picture and posed for it. You see, that was all quite a posed picture.

Q: Yes, and quite a picture.

Capt. L.: And it's amazing how many of those people were later admirals, which is a big percentage, really.

Q: A very large percentage.

Capt. L.: A very large percentage. Another member of that ship was Admiral Patrick. He was a year senior to the ones here. So we had quite a large percentage of people move on up the line, so I guess our training was pretty good.

Q: I'm sure it was sort of basic, at that point, wasn't it?

Capt. L.: Uh-huh. Well, those were the formative years, you know.

Q: All the other men have testified to that, I think. Now tell me about your relationships with Admiral Nimitz as the years went on. Where did you next see him?

Capt. L.: Well, the next time, I came back to - in 1936, I came back to join the USS Schenck, which was a four-stacker destroyer, and I went through Washington and I stopped to call on the family, and then I went to New Orleans and joined the ship, and then I was on the Schenck for 18 months. Then I came back to postgraduate school in Annapolis, and, of course, Annapolis is a short ways to Washington...

Q: And they were in Washington?

Capt. L.: They were in Washington at the time.

Q: What was he doing then?

Capt. L.: I think he was Assistant Chief of the Bureau of Navigation.

Q: Oh, I see, and this is when Catherine was...

Capt. L.: In the Music Library in the District Public Library. And she used to come down to Annapolis from time to time and...

Q: You had kept in touch with her?

Capt. L.: I'd kept in touch with her, and then during one summer while I was going to postgraduate school in Annapolis, I had duty in the Bureau of Ordnance. I'd taken ordnance postgraduate engineering course. And, of course, when I was in Washington, we used to play cribbage, and every Monday night was our night - we used to play cribbage every Monday night. Of course, we had other activities the rest of the week...

Q: But cribbage was with the family, was it?

Capt. L.: No, with Catherine. I used to play cribbage with Catherine. This was on Monday nights, and at that time, I guess- see, that was at 2222 Q Street, Catherine and Nancy had the back apartment and they had the front apartment on the same - in the same building, you see.

Q: I see.

Capt. L.: And one night, I'd picked Catherine up at the Library, we were going to play cribbage and I had about half a case of beer under my arm, and we met her parents in the elevator, you know, here was sticking out a case of beer under my...

Q: By that time, your romance had begun to blossom, I suspect?

Capt. L.: Well, actually, she was still interested in her career, and so I left the postgraduate school to go out to join the Louisville, and this was in 1941, so we didn't get married until 1945 because I spent the entire war in the Pacific. But I did see her father at Pearl Harbor from time to time, and, in fact, when Admiral Joy, who used to be commanding officer of the Louisville, he was Captain C. Turner Joy. Well, he used to take me along when he'd go to call on the Commander-in-Chief, Pacific...

Q: Because he knew of your connection?

Capt. L.: Yes. He knew I knew the family, so he would take me along, which was always nice.

Lay - 17

Q: Tell me about some of those calls during the war. Did you see him in any...?

Capt. L.: One very interesting day, we went up to pay our respects, I was with Admiral Joy, I guess, at the time, and we had been there about, oh, five minutes, and he said, "Pardon me, but I have an appointment. You just sit right here. That's all right." And here was a destroyer division coming through, and here were four brand-new destroyers, the skippers getting ready to go out and join the war, and he had an appointment and he was going to keep it with them. So they came in, all four of them, and he just talked to them like they were his sons, you know, and he was proud of them and they were going out and do a good job, he was sure, of this, and I'm sure they went away feeling like a million dollars. Here, they had pushed the captain aside while he kept his appointment with the commanders. But he would do this.

Q: Uh-huh. Were you with him at any time just before one of the crucial battles, or right after the crucial battle?

Capt. L.: Well, after two years, I joined the amphibious forces. I had been a gunnery officer, you see, while Admiral Conolly said he wanted a gunnery officer, and at that time I'd worked up though, I was first lieutenant damage control of the Louisville, and so the Bureau said, gee, here's a gunnery officer not doing gunnery duties. So he says, OK, I want him. So I was just coming back to - we were getting some radars put on the Louisville - coming in for overhaul, actually, we'd had our radars on last time, that's right - and so they flew me right back out to Pearl Harbor as soon as we got in. I didn't even get home on vacation or anything else, to join Admiral Connolly. Of course, I was with him for about six months, and I spent the last eighteen months of the war with Vice Admiral Wilkinson as his gunnery officer, Commander, Third Amphibious Force. Of course, in between operations we would base in Pearl Harbor, and so several times during this time, the Admiral would say, "Well, come on out and go swimming with me." So he and Admiral Spruance and maybe a couple of other staff officers we'd go out to the north side of the - of Oahu - and swimming was always quite a chore because he would walk down the beach about three miles, then we'd swim back. He'd get his walk and his swim in, and everybody said, "Boy, if you want your exercise, just go swimming with the Admiral."

Q: And if you couldn't make it, what would you do?

Capt. L.: Well, you had to - if you wanted to stop, you could stop and walk back, you see. But everybody figured, well, if the Admiral could do it, I can, too. But you would come back and really feel that you'd had your exercise. And this was his pattern, the way he took his exercise. You know, he'd take a nice long walk and a nice long swim.

Q: Were you with him at a crucial moment ever?

Capt. L.: No, not during the battles, because - of course, on amphibious operations we were always out, and when we went in to, let's see, what's the name of the one that we have out there...?

Q: Okinawa?

Capt. L.: Okinawa. Well, that was Admiral Turner's exercise, you see, and I was with Admiral Wilkinson, but I spent a week out there as an observer, and then when I flew off Okinawa, well, Admiral Nimitz was in Guam at that time, and I remember I got there late at night -- not too late, but I mean about dinner time -- and he said, "I'll save you a place for dinner." And so I arrived when everybody else was about ready to have dessert, but he still had a place at table for me to have dinner with him. I guess this was just after we were married, wasn't it? That's right because...

Q: Just after you were married?

Capt. L.: Just after, yeah, because we were married in March, and this was after, if I remember rightly, in '45. Wasn't that about May or June?

Q: Yes. Oh, you decided to be married even before the war was over?

Capt. L.: Yeah. I came back and, well, I'd sent Catherine a ring before, you see. Then I came back on one of these unexpected trips, and we came back to Washington for ten days, and we said, well, this might be a good time to get married. I took -- I guess we took a week off, and went up to the Cape, that's where I...

Q: Did he - you met Miss Freeman?

Capt. L.: Yes, and came back and it just so happened that we found out that Catherine's father was going to come back to Washington for some - that was just before Mary christened the Buck, I think it was, and they were supposed to leave on Saturday for Mary to christen the Buck, and we thought this would be a good time to get married, so we got married...

Q: So the Admiral was present?

Capt. L.: He was present, yes, they were present. They were going to leave later on that night, I guess. The next day, I guess it was, because - you know,, Washington had this three-day law - that's right because it was either going to be get married just after midnight on Thursday, to get in the third day, or Friday afternoon. It so happened, I think, the weather was good enough that they could go the next day, so we got married that day - on Friday.

Q: Were they delighted that the two of you finally decided...?

Capt. L.: I think they were, yes. Then I went back to the war and I didn't get back till October. We were steaming in to Tokyo Bay while the surrender was being signed.

Q: Oh, you were?

Capt. L.: Yeah, we were going by about a mile away in the

Lay - 21

<u>Mount Olympus</u>, the flagship of Vice Admiral Wilkinson, and so we were about a mile away, and so my boss didn't get over to the signing.

Q: And then, of course, after the war...

Capt. L.: Well, after the war, then - let's see, I left there, I guess it was the 20th of September and came back in, I think it was the <u>General Sturgis</u>, the transport, and we were supposed to come in to San Francisco, and Admiral Halsey brought the fleet back at that time, and so he was taking up all the San Francisco area, and they diverted us to Seattle. And I landed at Seattle, and meantime, Catherine had come out from Washington to San Francisco and was staying with some friends to meet me there and my car was in San Francisco and we were going to drive back across country. Well, I landed in Seattle and I flew down, because I was ordered back to the Bureau of Ordnance for duty there, and plane travel was almost impossible in those days. So I inquired and I said, well, my ticket says "travel by air back to Washington, how do I go?" And he said, "Well, you'll have to go MATS." And I said, "How does MATS go?" and they said, "Well, we leave Seattle and we go down to San Francisco, then from there back to Washington."

Q: And you can get bumped off!

Capt. L.: And I said, "Supposing I get off at San Francisco." They said, "That's perfectly all right with us." So, I took my first leg of the travel to San Francisco and joined Catherine

Lay - 22

in San Francisco. Then we drove back across country. Of course, in those days driving across country was quite a...

Q: Well, yes, it was quite a time-consuming thing, too.

Capt. L.: Time-consuming and also, well, you couldn't depend on accommodations. And I remember we came back to Salt Lake City - remember Salt Lake City after the war - and we had driven till almost dark, and every place we stopped there were no accommodations. So then we stopped in Salt Lake City, and no hotel, called all around and nobody had a place. So we said, oh, there are motels certainly on this side of Salt Lake City, so we started out and when after about 50 or 60 miles we decided we'd better stop for the night, so we slept in the car that night. We just couldn't find a place to stay. Cold! And so the next day we stopped early, it was in Colorado, I guess, the second day, and we stopped about 4 o'clock and had a nice cocktail and a hot bath.

Q: You had to be something of a pioneer to make a trip...

Capt. L.: Almost.

Q: Even at that time. Well, now, you were stationed in Washington when the Nimitzes were back there, when he was CNO?

Capt. L.: Yes. And we lived in Maryland, on Newport Avenue in Maryland [Bethesda], when he was at the Observatory. In fact, Jimmy was born in Washington while he was CNO.

Q: You saw them quite often then, in those days?

Capt. L.: Oh, yes. In fact, he'd walk out to our house

practically every Sunday, and we'd see them in between times, but they...

Q: Walk out from the Observatory?

Capt. L.: From the Observatory out to...

Q: Where, Bethesda?

Capt. L.: ~~No~~. You know where Spring Valley is?

Q: Oh, yes.

Capt. L.: Well, Newport Avenue is just out Wisconsin - River Road, you see.

Q: Yes.

Capt. L.: We were just off River Road, about a block, outside the District line. But they'd walk from the Observatory on Sunday morning, just for a walk.

Q: Then, of course, you'd have to walk them home.

Mrs. L.: What?

Q: You had to walk them home, to be courteous.

Mrs. L.: Oh, no. But he never missed a chance to walk.

Capt. L.: He loved to walk.

Mrs. L.: I used to feel sorry for the junior officers who rode in the car pool, because I'm sure they were quite disenchanted about this.

Capt. L.: Let's walk today, huh!

Mrs. L.: He'd stop at Sheridan Circle, and "everybody out."

Capt. L.: He'd walk back from the Navy Department up to Q Street.

Mrs. L.: We used to call back and forth- and we'd agree to meet and he'd call the Library at Dupont Circle very often.

Capt. L.: Yes. he'd walk all the way from Constitution Avenue to...

Mrs. L.: Then the buses got to the point where the fumes were so obnoxious-walking up Connecticut Avenue-that he gave it up, it was so unpleasant, but the distance was nothing.

Q: Tell me about the garden party that was given for Admiral Togo, Mrs. Lay, which happened when your father was quite a junior officer.

Mrs. L.: On the Ohio. I don't remember whether he was a passed midshipman or an ensign, but the fact is that there was an imperial garden party and the midshipmen were invited, and all these young men from the Ohio were sitting at one table and they were very anxious to go up and speak to Admiral Togo, but they didn't quite have the courage, and so they delegated Dad to go up and ask him if he would allow them to come up and meet him. And Togo very graciously got up and went over and sat with them and spoke to them and, I think, gave them his autograph. I thought this was rather a nice switch because in view of what happened with the Mikasa and all that afterwards.

Q: Yes, and your father's interest after World War II in...

Mrs. L.: Yes. He admired Admiral Togo very much.

Q: Well, Mrs. Lay, would you cast your mind back to your childhood days and tell me about some of the things that...

Mrs. L.: I think it's partially because I'm a librarian that the first recollection - really vivid recollection - that I have of Dad is in Honolulu when we both - Ches and I - were very young, was of his reading to us. We were read to constantly when we were growing up, both by Mother and Dad, but on this occasion we had...

Q: What was their purpose? Educational?

Mrs. L.: I don't think they had any purpose. They just thought it was a nice thing to do, as we thought it was a nice thing to do for our children. We weren't trying consciously to do anything. And we had chickenpox together, it was one of the few times that we ever were nice enough to do this at the same time, and I can remember my father sitting in a straight-back chair in the hall outside our two rooms on the ground floor of this house in the hills of Honolulu, and reading Robinson Crusoe to us. He read the whole thing from start to finish. The other book that he tried to read us on this occasion was an adaptation of Maeterlinck's Bluebird, which my great aunt from Cambridge had sent us. And he got halfway - oh, not even halfway – into it and just couldn't stand it, and now that I'm grown up I think he had impeccable taste; I hate it myself. But he did, both he and Mother read to us, and I had several eye operations later, when I was in junior high school, and he read me all The Count of Monte Cristo and, of course, he read all the Thornton Burgess to us – he must have hated that, but he was a good reader and he enjoyed doing this, and a lot of these things he was reading for the first time himself, I think, the longer ones. But I can still see that Robinson Crusoe with the footprints across the cover, you know, the big thick dark green edition, which is no longer available, I'm sure, but it was the full unexpurgated, uncut version. That's about the only memory I have...

Q: But those must be delightful memories...

Mrs. L.: Of Honolulu? Well, you know, he was really wonderful with kids...

Q: Did your mother sit in also, and listen?

Mrs. L.: I think Mother was probably upstairs looking after Nancy. Very often she read to us. I should say it was – we never went to bed without being read to, and it was sort of a, just automatic thing. And this continued even to the time when Mary was growing up. I think by that time, Dad was reduced to reading Ferdinand to her, and she had memorized it, and every time he missed a comma, she protested. Then from Honolulu, we came to Newport, where Dad was going to the War College...

Q: Is your house still here?

Mrs. L.: Yes. They rented a ghastly ark on Hunter Avenue. Eight bedrooms, a butler's pantry, a scullery, a range in the kitchen that you could have cooked for the Hotel Viking on, and it had been a summer house and it had been very inexpertly converted to winter use, and we never even went up on the third floor. There were four bedrooms and a bath up there, probably for servants originally. And they burned 20 tons of coal - that's their memory of Newport - that winter. There was a coal strike, and Dad used to get coal at the commissary in grocery bags. So when Jay and I found that we were coming up to Newport, when he got his job with Raytheon, I said jokingly, you know, over the telephone, "Who knows, we may end up at 55 Hunter Avenue," and they were each on a different telephone and they both said, "Oh, God, not that house."

Q: It's still standing then?

Mrs. L.: Oh, yes, it is, and Skipper, my cousin, Uncle Otto's son, lived about two doors from there when he was at Newport. And I didn't find out till years later that my father's thesis at the War College had been on the Battle of Jutland, and I found this out unhappily when I was in junior high school, when he was in Berkeley, and I remarked one night when we were clearing off the table, that I had to go and do a report on the Battle of Jutland, and this was just like putting gasoline on a fire. When I came back with the J Volume of the Encyclopedia Britannica, he had the dining room table all cleared, and he always left it set for breakfast. You know, he was very efficient about these things. He always set it for breakfast the night before. So I said, "What's the matter?" He said, "Er, don't you have to do a report on the Battle of Jutland?" And I said, "Oh, yes, half a page," and I had the J volume. "Well," he said, "I'll tell you about the Battle of Jutland." And afterwards, all I could think of in later years, you know, the old story about "Thank you for the book, it taught me more about penguins than I wanted to know." We had salt cellar and pepper shakers, and the German High Seas Fleet was here and the British Fleet here. We went through this, and I was weakly saying, "Half a page." But I never forgot this and I never brought up the Battle of Jutland again. And when Jim was in high school here, he had to do a paper on it, and I said, "Oh, too bad your grandfather isn't here." At a book sale later on, I met a very charming lady here, who is now the librarian at de la Salle, she was the librarian at the War College, and she came up and spoke to me, and said, "Oh, you know, we still have your father's thesis on file at the War College. I wonder if you know what it was?" And I said, Oh, yes, I know.

Q: During that period here, your mother had lots of chores on her own, didn't she?

Mrs. L.: At Newport? Well, I guess, when you have a house like that and three children in school, you do. We had every childhood disease that we hadn't had before that winter, and I just - I do remember that we started school at Punahoe, Chester and I, and we went barefoot. Went out of the back door - was like a little country town in Honolulu in the 1920s, just like a country town - and we went out of the back door of this house and over a hill through a cow pasture, and turned down into the back gate of Punahoe, and when we came back to Newport, it would have been in August, I suppose, because the War College starts then, it never crossed our minds that you had to wear shoes to school, and when we found that this was expected, we were very unhappy. I guess we would have given up on this in November, probably - on the barefoot idea - but we found this was quite a bitter pill to swallow. We were here just one year and I really don't remember too much more about it.

Q: Your mother said that she was awfully happy to get away from Newport.

Mrs. L.: I thought of it as a very dark town. Of course, in the summer when the trees are out, there are certain streets, like Hunter Avenue, where it's really brooding. I mean, it's stark and overpowering, and we went just one year to the nearest local grammar school, but I have no other memories. And I think we went from here to San Pedro.

Q: But before you did, your brother almost died, didn't he?

Mrs. L.: Oh, he was always - a real "calamity Joe." That's when we were just ready to leave by train for San Pedro and he fell off the top of the garage at my grandparents' and fractured his skull. So we did later go out to San Pedro by train and I - no, we went on a steamer, I guess, we went on a transport, and on the transport he managed to burn his leg on a steam pipe. He was always breaking something or banging something up. And I really don't remember too much about San Pedro except, you know, loads and loads of walks and this overweight bulldog that Dad had and Admiral Robertson had [Robison (ss)] another overweight bulldog, Mac, and they used to talk the dogs in the San Pedro hills, and very often either Mac or Polly would just simply pass out and have to be carried home. It was a most unattractive town in those days. They'd had some kind of a boom and I remember many - there were many half-built houses in the area that we lived in that had simply been left with the foundations only, an oil boom or something, and, of course, Dad was gone most of the time. And I think we were there, what, about a year and a half while he was on the California.

Q: He really applied himself to his career, didn't he?

Mrs. L.: I guess he did. I was never conscious of this while growing up. I never thought of him as being ambitious or, you know, consciously ambitious, but I wouldn't have, you know, I don't think children do, particularly. He never struck me as - I think the Navy was his whole life, in fact, I know it was, but I never felt, consciously felt, that he was really working at furthering his career in that sense. I think that when he went to Berkeley, when he was at the ROTC, that those were three of the pleasantest years of their Navy duty, and I think one of the...

Q: Focus on them, will you?

Mrs. L.: Well, I think one of the things that, even as a very young child, that I was aware of was that this was the first time that they had been exposed to a largely non-Navy group, where there were a lot of experts in their own field; obviously there were a lot of wonderful "kooks", and they really enjoyed meeting all of these people who were in different fields. On the other hand, the aspects of university life that amuse a lot of people, amused Dad and sort of horrified him, like the "publish or perish" bit and, oh, he used to be horrified at the thesis subjects. He would read about that and come home and tell us, "Do you realize that I read that somebody had written a thesis today on such - or had a thesis on such-and-such a subject." He thought some of the topics were pretty ridiculous.

Q: Not very practical, huh?

Mrs. L.: Well, yes, and - I remember one instance. It was very easy to get babysitters there because they had all these students working their way through college, and one night he and mother were going out to a dinner party and the University employment office sent them a Miss Lake - I remember her name. She was rather large, she was getting her Ph.D., and we had an old Atwater Kent radio, and after we children went to bed, she apparently sat up and played the radio and left it on. Of course, by the time the family got home there were no programs going, and so the next morning Dad discovered that the radio battery was dead, and all he could say was, "Here's a candidate for a Ph.D. and she doesn't have any common sense at all." But we lived on a street which was almost entirely professors, on Bayview Place, and a very interesting and heterogeneous group of people lived there.

Q: That must have been good for him, though.

Mrs. L.: Oh, I think it was wonderful, and of course he loved the university and was delighted when - I mean that was the only place I was going to go. I mean he had that all planned. I was in my junior year at high school when he left Berkeley and I went back East for one year of high school, but there was just no question but that I was coming back to go to the university. He was very much impressed with it. And he and mother went to lots of - there were always lectures and concerts and things going on - and they really did enjoy this. It's a lovely city to live in, even now when it's built up.

Q: And he obviously found great pride in building up the ROTC.

Mrs. L.: Oh, yes. Yes. Oh, one thing that I remember very distinctly. When he first started correcting students' papers, (you know, Nancy had said and I think this was very true, that Dad would have made an excellent editor) He had a wonderful ear for redundancy, and he spoke and wrote really very unadorned, but impeccable, English, and this is quite rare today, I've decided. The language is going to pot. *

Q: You're so right.

* Mrs L. is a perfect example, if this is an accurate transcript

Mrs. L.: And I can remember him sitting and correcting blue books and saying in disgust, "Listen to this - the lifeboats should be lowered as immediately as possible," and snorting, you know. He was just unprepared for this sloppiness of language, and he did, I think, write very concisely and when he worked on the Naval Institute <u>Proceedings</u> as an editor, he was on the Board and he used to read manuscripts, Nancy and I used to read some of the manuscripts, and we always enjoyed his comments. He would have been a good editor. He wrote wonderful letters to us, really wonderful, and he wrote us all the time, even during the war.

Q: Letters that said things?

Mrs. L.: Yeah. The letters that Mother and I were reading at Treasure Island that he wrote to his family were lovely letters that you'd love to get from your son, and the letters they wrote back to him were so completely unimaginative and sort of joyless, you know. They didn't seem to enjoy him the way he enjoyed us. Both he and Mother have always given all of us the feeling they were enormously proud of us; they'd smack you down if you got out of line, but I mean they always were very supportive and tried to give us selfconfidence, to let us know that they were proud of us and, I think, partly because he didn't get this - I'm sure he didn't from these letters. It just seems obvious, you know, very stern, no nonsense. I hope you have some of those letters...

Q: Well, his family represented a different kind of culture.

Lay - 34

Mrs. L.: Absolutely. That's right. They did. I didn't - of course, my memories of Grandmother Nimitz are, as I say, of a person who sent us wonderful boxes of cookies. I think the last time I saw her myself, I was six and I couldn't have told you what she looked like. I have pictures of her as a young girl, she was gorgeous, but I don't remember her at all, except as a rather slight and elderly person. And my grandfather - my step grandfather - as I remember was rather fat with quite a German accent. He came up to Wollaston, when I graduated from the eighth grade. I don't know how he happened to do this, but he came up and stayed with my grandmother and grandfather. He was there for my graduation, came down to the Cape and spent a weekend with us. That's the only time I saw him. He used to call Nancy Anna, which was her name, of course. She was named for his wife, and at that point Nancy didn't want to be called Anna. She became very fond of the name after she got involved with Slavic literature, decided it was a nice name, but at that point she'd say, "I won't answer him." But I have very little, very few...

Q: You did know your Uncle Otto?

Mrs. L.: Yes, I did.

Q: Tell me about him.

Mrs. L.: Well, I say I knew him. They visited us on several occasions. They had one child, Skipper, and he (Otto) was very different from Dad, both in looks and in temperament. He was a stern father.

Q: Germanic type?

Mrs. L.: Yeah, very - don't argue, no nonsense, and Skipper just adored the ground Dad walked on, because, as I say, Dad just loved all kids, and he was very fond of Skipper. Skipper's out of the Navy now and living in Virginia Beach, and grew up to be one of the nicest people in the world and married a lovely girl, and they have four boys, all of whom are just beautiful. We knew them in Arlington quite well. That was the first time we'd really had a chance to know him. I think the last time I saw Uncle Otto was in Arlington, he and Aunt Louisa were at Q Street. I don't remember the occasion.

Q: He's been dead for quite a long time, hasn't he?

Mrs. L.: Er - since Chet got out of the Navy.

Q: Oh, in the '50s?

Mrs. L.: Yeah. And Aunt Louisa was down in Texas.

Q: Was your father close to him in these latter years?

Mrs. L.: No. They were never very close, I don't think. They were just different temperamentally. He was Dad's half-brother.

Q: The same mother, but...

Mrs. L.: Yeah.

Q: What rank did he achieve?

Mrs. L.: What did he, Jay? Captain? Commander?

Capt. L.: Captain, I think. Yeah, I think he retired as a captain. ~~overseas~~ (Inaudible)

Mrs. L.: Well, I guess the next place that I remember vividly is the Riegal [Risel] in ~~San Pedro~~ San Diego, when Dad had the destroyer base.

Q: Oh, when you lived on board ship?

Mrs. L.: I was gone most of the time, at the university, but he took over the Riegal [Risel] when I was a sophomore, the same — practically the same day that Mary was born. I hope they told you the story about the 25th Anniversary Yearbook that his class put out, you know, as they very often do. <u>Twentyfive Years After</u>, I think it was called.

Q: No, they didn't.

Mrs. L.: Dad's biography, very brief, characteristically very understated, but he said, "My third and last child, Nancy, is in junior high school," and it wasn't but about a week or so after this book came out that we found that there was going to be another, and of course we really gave it to him. "My third and last child," and all his classmates would walk into a woom and they'd say, "My third and last child." And she was born just about the day Dad took over the Riegal [Risel], and I'm sure Mother and Nancy have told you, Mary was brought up by the entire destroyer base. Anybody in uniform was Daddy, it didn't matter, admiral on down. It was just like the dogs and cats on the base. They barked at people who weren't in uniform. Mary wept when anyone [not in uniform] came near her, and she had a playpen out on the deck and everybody who went by - no babysitter. Everybody who went by talked to her and this was...

Q: That was really the Nimitz ship, wasn't it?

Mrs. L.: That was lovely. Oh, but I do have a lovely anecdote about the Riegal [Rigel]. Did Mother tell you about the midshipmen's full-dress uniform and the Eleventh Naval District ball? I used to babysit for them...

Q: No. Do tell me about it.

Mrs. L.: When I would come home from college. I was home - this was the summer after Mary was born, she was only a year. And Mother and Dad were going to a formal, full-dress Eleventh Naval District ball - I don't know what the occasion was - and it was an after dinner thing. They were dressed for the ball. We had dinner on the ship and Dad was saying - you know he was always very much interested in physical fitness - and he was saying, "I want you to know this is my midshipman's full-dress uniform. I've just had the gold braid changed, and I don't think there are many captains who could get into their midshipman's full-dress uniform." And I'm saying, "That's wonderful." Well, they went off to the ball, Mary went to bed, and I sat up reading a detective story, finally I went to sleep, and the Riegal [Rigel] had iron decks, so you could never sneak on board after curfew, because it - every footfall just rang - clang, clang...

Q: Like a creaky stair.

Mrs. L.: Right. I could hear my mother giggling as they came down the step toward the cabin, and they swept in the door, and Dad went right thru the dining room and into their bedroom, and my Mother is just absolutely in hysterics. I said, "What's so funny?" Well, she could hardly pull herself together to tell me that Mrs. Senn, the Admiral's wife, Commandant of the Eleventh Naval District, had dropped her lorgnette early in the ball, and my father had leaned over to pick it up, and had split his trousers right up the rear and had spent the rest of the evening against the wall. Dad, well, he had enough of a sense of humor, so the next morning he was thinking this was pretty funny, too, and at breakfast he said to Mother, "Im going to call up Mrs. Senn and I'm going to tell her that this gesture of chivalry has cost me $90." So my Mother said, "You are not going to do any such thing." Well, when we were stationed in Coronado, years later, and Admiral Senn had been gone for a long time, we were invited to a cocktail party at the Murphys', and Mrs. Senn, very much the dowager empress, was seated on the couch and it was sort of understood that everybody would come up and take a turn speaking to her. So I came up, sat down, and I didn't know whether anybody had ever told her this story, and she was really a very dignified person. My mother used to say, "She is the personification of the admiral's wife," and I used to believe this until my Mother got to be an admiral's wife and I thought, well, she's different. And so I told her this story which, you know, I thought was very funny, and she was absolutely not amused.

Q: She wasn't?

Mrs. L.: She was not amused. I couldn't wait to get out of there. Well, I do think that probably - you know, Admiral Jackson at the age of, what, 90 something, went to a ball wearing his midshipman's full-dress uniform...

Q: Did he really?

Mrs. L.: Of course, he's tiny and I guess he hadn't gained an ounce.

Q: He's 103 now.

Mrs. L.: What a man.

Q: Nearly 104.

Mrs. L.: Yeah. But that's one of my more vivid memories of... and the other thing was, we could entertain our friends just by - we'd go over and watch them put a ship up on the marine railway, ride out with it and ride back, or there were 35, at that time, decommissioned destroyers moored side by side, and that was always interesting, to walk your friends out to the outboard destroyer. There were so many things to do down there that, I mean, you didn't have to entertain anybody. Just walk them around the base, and Mary, as I say, just was so spoiled. By the time she left there, and then they went to China where she had an amah, and by the time she came back from China there was just absolutely no living with her, you know.

Q: That's likely to happen with a child so late, too.

Mrs. L.: Yeah. Well, I stayed - and Chet was at the Naval Academy, he did get home on leave and he had the cabin up on the - was it the chart house, yeah. And you know the person who did the quarters over, the man who had them before Dad, his wife had hired a decorator and it was full of stars and the bunks were built in and had curtains, and everything was very...

Q: This was on the Rigel?

Mrs. L.: Yes, on the Rigel. Very lush, plush. And we had a cat on the base, named Curio, that they encouraged to live on the Rigel because we really did have a rat problem, and Curio distinguished herself by having seven kittens under the table during a dinner party, and these kittens my brother was absolutely enchanted with, and I can see him now staying in bed till late, but he had all the kittens up there in the ?chart house and he would jiggle curtains in his bunk and make the kittens climb up into the bunk. You'd go up there about 11 o'clock and he was in bed with all these kittens. We really did have a rat problem, though, and the rat guards didn't seem to do any good on the ropes, and every once in a while they'd fumigate the ship and then they'd die in the compartments and that was just jolly.

Q: That must have been upsetting to your mother, wasn't it?

Mrs. L.: Oh, I don't think she worried about it too much. Besides the rats, our dog Polly used to go over and she'd get these very, very defunct oysters off the bottom of the ships from the marine railway and bring those home and bury them, you know, either at the foot of somebody's bed or in a corner. Nancy, I know, must have told you that she spent all of her time in the machine shop. She was really - she was another pet on the base, I mean, she was very competent with tools, even then, and was always over in the carpenter's shop or the machine shop. I can remember my mother coming home very disgustedly because she'd been walking round the base with Mary, and one of the petty officer's had said, "You know, Nancy runs a better acetylene well than any of the men in the shop." And Mother said, "That's just lovely."

Q: Meanwhile, you were pursuing your education?

Mrs. L.: I was at Cal, at home only on the - on vacations. I used to run back and forth on the old Harvard and Yale, and then the Harvard ran aground. Then they ran the poor old Yale back and forth from San Francisco to to Wilmington, and then you had to take the electric train into Los Angeles, and then the bus from Los Angeles down. That was the last two years. Those ships were so ancient and creeky even when - they had carried troops in the First World War, I believe. They had chevrons on the stacks. First, they used to run between Boston and New York, then they carried troops overseas during World War I.

Q: Was your father closely interested in your progress, your education?

Mrs. L.: Very. Oh, yes, very much, and of course he had...

Q: How did he show this?

Mrs. L.: Well, he had many friends still on the faculty, and, well, he showed it - I was of course majoring in English and French, which were - had I chosen to major in math he would have been happier, I guess, but I would never have gotten to college if he hadn't helped me with algebra and geometry, which I loathe. I can't say I've anything to do with math or science to this day. But he was interested in everything that we did. He really...

Q: Did he have some kind of career in mind for you, or did he...?

Mrs. L.: No, he didn't. I think when I started taking zoology, he and Mother both had some crazy idea that I might want to become a doctor. Nothing could have been further from my thoughts. I loathed everything to do with it. And I guess he either hoped I would become a musician, which I was not very good at - we all played, but - or that I would write, you know after. There was nothing we couldn't do, you know, as far as he was concerned. As Nancy's told you, he was very, very fond of music. I've saved some of his annotated symphony programs. He used to send me the programs of the San Francisco Symphony Orchestra. He was very fond of Beethoven and Mozart and of Schubert and the nineteenth century - lovely big orchestral things. He didn't like modern music too much, and he would send me these annotated symphony programs. Sometimes he graded the piece 2.5, 4.0 or "lousy." I've got one here in which opposite the Beethoven Seventh, he's written "lovely, my favorite." Then opposite a modern symphony, he's written, "First, probably last performance of this work." I often thought I should have saved them for the Library of Congress music division, because they were very interested in Dad because I was music librarian at the District of Columbia library and saw a great deal of the LC people.

Q: He didn't play any instrument...?

Mrs. L.: He didn't play - well, for one thing, you see, he had this missing finger. He was so fond of music though that he would sit with this happy smile and listen to Nancy and me practising or crucifying four-hand music. We were always banging on the piano. He loved to listen to records, and I know that when he was in Washington as Assistant Chief of the Bureau of Navigation and we lived out in Chevy Chase, there was a program called "Today's Prelude," we always woke up to "Today's Prelude." And at Berkeley, Chester was taking violin lessons and I was taking piano lessons and when the alarm went off at 6 o'clock Dad would stand at the foot of the stairs and wake us up. He'd go out in the kitchen and squeeze a big glass of orange juice for us, and then we were supposed to get in half an hour's practising before breakfast, Chet upstairs and I downstairs, and I must say Chester and I are very, very good friends now, but we had some absolutely mortal hand-to-hand combats with our music because we were expected to play together, and when we had a discussion about the tempo, it wasn't just a discussion at all, it ended up with somebody picking up something to fling at somebody.

Q: Of course.

Mrs. L.: It must have stood him in good stead in his World War II training, you know, all this hand-to-hand combat he had with me.

Q: But your father actually fostered this 6.30 practice, ...

Mrs. L.: Yeah, and really - I mean he'd sit and read the paper and beam while I practised Czerny finger exercises. He just loved to hear music on a piano. And he - I think - well, when he would come up to San Francisco when I was in college, if the fleet were up there, he'd, you know, take me out to dinner. We'd awlays go to a concert if there were anything on in San Francisco, and there usually was. Not opera particularly, but...

Q: No, he really didn't like the opera, did he?

Mrs. L.: No. He didn't like anything that kept him sitting still too long, and he really disliked modern music. He was very fond of Sidney Griller, of the Griller Quartet. They lived up the street from Dad, and through Sidney, he was exposed to a great deal of modern music. On one occasion, they played a Bloch Quartet and then they played something conservative in the middle, and then they repeated the Bloch, something that a lot of modern musicians have done. It's a very good idea, but Dad took his program and wrote on it, drew a block of type and said, "You've heard the expression 'two blocks', you know what that means, Sidney? I've had it."

Q: Well, now, the rest of the family ~~all prefer your mother's taste?~~

Mrs. L.: We all play. Mother used to sing beautifully and we all played, and we played together. Mary played viola. We all played piano at one time. Chester when he went to - he married a girl whose mother is a wonderful musician - and...

Q: She's a concert...

Mrs. L.: Yes, and she got Chester going on his violin again, to the point that when he went to Korea, you know, when he left for Korea he took his violin with him, and his division commander threatened him, "If you don't stop practising Sevcik, I'm going to send home for my trumpet." But he and Joan then started playing together again. Everybody was enjoying it, you know. We're none of us any good.

Q: All except your father!

Mrs. L.: Yeah. Well, I think he never had the opportunity originally, and then there was no instrument that he could have played with this...

Q: Did he have much of a voice for singing?

Mrs. L.: No. I do remember when we were young that he used to sing "Away, away, with sword and rum, Here I come full of rum," for us. But I wouldn't say that he had a voice.

Q: Would you tell me about that period when he was in Washington as Assistant Chief of the Bureau - it was the Bureau of Navigation, wasn't it?

Mrs. L.: That was what it was, then, and we had just come back from China...

Q: And you were in the...

Mrs. L.: I was in library school, and went to work in the District of Columbia Library and then, actually, the war came along - well, I guess he went out to the - what was the ship he was on - went out to the West Coast, he and Mother - and then they had come back to Washington.

Capt. L.: Was it the Arizona he was on?

Mrs. L.: Yeah. The Trenton and then the Arizona.

Capt. L.:   the battleship division?

Mrs. L.: Yeah. ComDesBat 4, or something. And when they went out to the West Coast, I was going to have an apartment, anyway. I was over 21 and I was going to do this, and we talked them into letting Nancy, who was a junior at George Washington and an excellent student, share the apartment. So we had actually ten years in Washington, and the two of us in this apartment had a marvellous time. And they were briefly out - it seemed to me a very short time - out on the West Coast, and then they came back, it would have been just before the war, and got an apartment in our apartment building...

Q: And then he was Chief of the Bureau...?

Mrs. L.: And then he was Chief of the Bureau, and after Pearl Harbor, it was a very short time before he was sent out to Honolulu, and the day that he found out he was going to go out, he came home and told Mother, and Nancy and I used to eat our meals with them across the hall, and we came in for supper that night and he said, "Now, I have some news, but this is not for publication." And Nancy and I said with one breath, "You are going out to Pearl Harbor." And Mother said, "I told you that they would guess this." And he was expecting to be approached by the press, and he sat at dinner and he took a 3 x 4 pad like this, and he was thinking of something that he could write, some statement that he could give to the press, and he finally wrote a sentence and tore off the paper and passed it around the table, and said, "Does this sound all right?" And he had said, "It is a great responsibility, and I will do my utmost to meet it." We all agreed that this was very good, so I tore it off and put it in my pocket, and I said, "I'm sure this is history," so make another copy," so he made another copy, and Nancy tore that one off and said, "I'll keep that one." And then Joan, who was Joan Nimitz then, said, "My copy." So he ended up by writing it four times before he got one he could keep.

Q: Did he give that to the press?

Mrs. L.: He gave that one to the press, and I think that was the statement that he made. Then - did Nancy tell you about the cablegram that we sent him the first Father's Day of the war? We were perpetually impoverished in our library jobs because we would go down and spent all of our money on records the day after pay day, and you know, things were still...

Q: 78s, huh?

Mrs. L.: Yes, 78s - still pretty grim out in the Pacific, and we decided we'd like to send him a nice cheery Father's Day cablegram - couldn't send him a telegram - and right across from the library, in the bank building, there was an office of the Mackay Cable Company. We'd never sent a cable in our lives. So we composed a rather warm Father's Day message and went over there, and the first thing we found out was that you had to pay not only for the message but for every word in the address, and it had to be very explicit. We couldn't see why it couldn't just say "Nimitz, Pacific," you know, but they couldn't do it that way, and also your complete signature and your address - 30 cents a word. And we totted this all up, and we couldn't do it, not with what we had. So we were sort of sadly leaving the office when the girl at the desk said, "Of course, you could send a deferred cable." And we said, "Well, what does that mean?" And she said, "Well, that won't go through for 24 hours." Well, this was Friday, and Father's

Day was Sunday, so we said, "Oh, that's marvellous, but how much is a deferred cable?" And they said, "15 cents a word." So we finally ended up with a rhyme, "We love you, Father, by cable deferred, even at 15 cents a word," which he got the biggest kick out of, and wrote us back, you know, everybody in the family thinks it is doggerel, I won't call it poetry, and I found this the other day when I was looking through a whole bunch of stuff I happened to be looking at here. But anyway he had written us a quatrain back about how our message by cable deferred had caught up with

I don't know where it is now, but he got a big kick out of that.

Q: Could only afford the 15-center. Well, going back to the time when he was here, when he was in Washington as the Assistant Chief of Bureau, are there any recollections of him in that time which stand out?

Mrs. L.: One of the things that I do remember is that, at that time, there was an investigation - quite an indignation - about naval officers who tried to further their careers by getting themselves repeatedly sent back to Washington, and Dad loathed Washington. For one thing, neither he nor I could stand hot weather, and for another thing, he just didn't like Washington that much. And at the time my grandmother died, my Mother had gone up to Massachusetts and Dad and I were keeping house together. I was about to get my library degree, and Nancy and all the rest of them had gone up to the Cape. And he was appearing on the Hill every day at these hearings, and it was just hotter than the hinges, you know, and he'd come back and regale me with how he had told them he didn't understand, he'd never heard of anybody who'd tried to get himself sent back to Washington, he simply could not understand anyone being that silly, because he didn't like it himself and he couldn't imagine anyone else liking it.

Q: That was in the days before air-conditioning.

Mrs. L.: Oh. Yes, but the other thing at this same time - my grandmother died just after Chester graduated, and Mother had planned to have a lot of goings and comings of Chester's classmates and so forth at the house in Washington, and she'd got an enormous canned ham, and then this all had to be called off. And she went off leaving Dad and me with this mammoth ham, and at that time I didn't know anything about cooking, I just sliced it and served it, you know, every meal doggedly. It didn't dawn on me you could put it - it would have kept. And we had it night after night after night. Then, the Canagas invited us out to dinner and we had ham. And I remember we sent a message to Mother, "Visit the Old Nimitz Homestead during Ham week." Oh, I never wanted to see another ham, absolutely never.

Q: Wasn't your father tempted to take a ham and and...

Mrs. L.: No. This was another thing about Dad - he was wonderful about - very concerned about housekeeping. I mean, whatever you put down, that was absolutely the best meal. Whatever you served him, he always told my Mother, this was a wonderful dinner, you know, and he knew that I wasn't any great shakes as a housekeeper, and I'd cook a vegetable and make a salad and fling this ham on the table. Then, oh - at that same time - I had been assistant chief of the music division, and I had never really expected to be made chief of it - this was supposed to be an interim job while they looked around...

Q: Was this the Public Library on 7th Street?

Mrs. L.: Right. ...while they looked around for a person who had the proper qualifications, and then one day when I was leaving work I found in my mail box official notification that the Librarian had decided that the time had come when I was going to be made chief of the music division and so forth. So I floated home on the bus and Dad was cutting the lawn - another very hot day...

Q: Did you say this was P Street?

Mrs. L.: No, this was when they were living in Chevy Chase.

Q: Where in Chevy Chase?

Mrs. L.: On Kirk Street - not Kirk Street, 39th Street, 5515 39th, in this half - duplex house - and I said, "Oh, what do you think? I've been given the job permanently." And the next day - oh, he was just so very delighted - the next day my boss, who was a rather prim New England type, said, "Oh, Miss Nimitz, what did your father say when you told him that you were the new chief of the music division?" And I said,

"Oh, he was very pleased." I didn't dare tell her that he had reached in his pocket and handed me five dollars and said, "Run round the corner and get a bottle of gin and we'll celebrate." That would not have done at all.

Q: No.

Mrs. L.: Of course, that library at 7th and K, you know the area, was out of bounds to military personnel during World War II. I'm talking about the area right behind it.

Q: I know it now.

Mrs. L.: Part of the worst, absolutely the worst area in town. Never a dull moment. Oh, one funny thing that happened, I don't think this is anything for your record, is that, this was also while he was Assistant Chief - there was a naval officer who was on the suspects list - this was about the time of Farnsworth and all the other selling of military secrets - but this man had married a Japanese woman while they were out in Pearl Harbor. Mother and Dad had known them briefly out there. And Naval Intelligence was looking for him. He had come back to Washington, or was reported to be in the area, and Dad used to get a certain amount of pleasure out of needling, I think it was Captain Puleston, who was at ONI then, about...

Q: Who?

Mrs. L.: Puleston, I think it was.

Mrs. L.: Puleston, I think it was.

Q: Oh, Puleston.

Mrs. L.: Yes. "Come out from behind the potted palm" you know, "we can see you." And he remarked at dinner one night to Mother, "You remember that odd ball old fellow who was out in Honolulu, you know the one that married the Japanese wife and everybody thought was a little strange. Well, the ONI is looking for him, and they know he's in the area somewhere and they can't find him." And about two nights later, I was on the registration desk at the Public Library and this man came up and said he wanted to get a library card and I gave him a blank to fill out, and he wrote his name, and I recognized it immediately, and I said, "Have you some identification?" He had given his rank as lieutenant commander, and he said, "No. Why should I?" And I said, "Oh, well, you'll be in here." And I turned round and reached for the Blue Book, you know, and he said, "I'm retired." I said, "Oh, but you'll still be in here." He got very indignant, but...

Q: You were much too knowledgeable.

Mrs. L.: Well, anyway, he filled out his registration blank and after he left I copied the address out, and went home, and I said, "I've found your friend for you." Dad went down the next morning and said to ONI, "Well, Catherine has found so-and-so for you. He's living out in southeast Washington." I don;t think anything ever came of it. I never heard that he was actually caught as a malefactor, but they were looking for him. We saw everybody up there at the registration desk at the Public Library, sonner or later.

Q: Was your father concerned, at that time, about developments in the Pacific? Did he talk about that at all?

Mrs. L.: I think he was always aware, don't you, Jay? I think he always felt that a conflict was - I think he felt this inevitable, sooner or later. I remember when we were in China and we were going through the grounds of the Temple of Heaven in Pekin, and there was all this rubble, you know, and Dad, who did have a tendency to throw out a remark just to see what the reaction would be, said to the guard, "Be pretty nice when the Japanese come in here and clean all this up, won't it?" And Nancy, and Mother, and I went, "Oh." And the guard said, "Japanese no can come." But, you know, it was already very obvious at the time we were out there. We spent the summer in Unzen and they opened our mail all summer long. We thought this was just funny, but that was quite a summer. That was the summer that - of the purge in Germany, and...

Q: That was '33?

Mrs. L.: '34. And we had a radio over in Unzen, but there was artificial sttic so you couldn't get any music from Harbin or any of the good Russian stations, you know. And Dad was on summer maneuvers in the Augusta and he used to write Mother almost every day, and we'd always get the letters the ends would be sandpaperd, and a couple of times Mother said something to the Post Office and they just blandly denied this, and the missionary in the next cottage said, "Don't bother. Last summer somebody got a letter from Italy and a letter from Germany in the same mail, and the German letter was in the Italian envelope and vice versa."

Q: Got them mixed up!

Mrs. L.: Yeah. I really feel that this is all very trivial, you know.

Q: Did they do a lot of entertaining of naval people in the time when they were in Washington?

Mrs. L.: I don't think they ever did very much formal entertaining until he was at the Observatory. They entertained all the time, just casually. People came to call and they always were invited to stay to dinner. Oh, they had a dinner party occasionally, but I mean most of it was, I think, unpremeditated and very informal. There was always plenty for another couple. I think they had the class of 1903 cocktail party the year that we were at 5515 in Chevy Chase, but I don't think - there was always partying, but I don't think of it as formal entertaining, you know. At the Observatory it was.

Q: It had to be.

Mrs. L.: Yeah.

Q: You were still there when he came back as Chief of the Bureau, weren't you?

Mrs. L.: Let's see.

Capt. L.: You were living with Nancy then.

Mrs. L.: Oh, yes. That's right. That's when Jay was at PG school, and that's when we started going out together.

Q: Getting serious?

Mrs. L.: Yes.

Capt. L.: That's when your folks wanted (7.)

Q: Then you were living on P Street?

Mrs. L.: Q Street, 2222 Q, of all the funny sounding addresses, and they had an apartment across the hall, and we had a very good time together.

Q: Well, by that time, it was becoming quite apparent that something was going to happen.

Mrs. L.: Oh, yes, and the day after Pearl Harbor - that was on a Sunday - and I always worked Monday nights, 1.30 to 9.00, and so Mother asked me to take Freckles to walk. Everybody was, you know, running around frantically. So I walked up Massachusetts Avenue and they were burning the papers in the Japanese Embassy, and there were photographers up in the tress, as you know, and I didn't have Freckles on a leash because he was very well behaved. And, of, to my horror, he rushed right into the middle of Japanese Embassy lawn. He had never done such a thing in his life before, and proceeded to misbehave, and I came back and I said to Mother, "There's all the press up there, and if they only knew they could write a headline 'Admiral's Dog Hurls Defiance at Nippon.'" We didn't hear a sound. The photographers were perched up in the trees and there was quite a crowd, and you could see all this smoke.

Q: I remember the newspaper picture of the smoke.

Capt. L.: Catherine chasing Freckles across the lawn.

Mrs. L.: Oh, that dog! That lovely dog! He was the most rank-conscious creature that ever breathed, after he realized that he was an admiral's dog.

Q: Tell me something more of your father's reactions to his assignment, other than the message for the press.

Mrs. L.: I really was not - I can't remember that he had anything else to say.

Q: How about your Mother?

Mrs. L.: Oh, I think Mother was, you know, a mixture of pride but very much concerned, too. Chet was already out there on a submarine, somewhere. We didn't know where he was. We just knew he was out in the Pacific somewhere. It's funny, but I really don't remember that she had too much to say. She just knew that he was going out.

Q: And he really didn't have very much time, did he?

Mrs. L.: No.

Q: To wind up his affairs.

Mrs. L.: He didn't.

Q: Why did he choose to go incognito, and...

Mrs. L.: I don't know whether that was his choice or not, or whether he was instructed. I know he went out as Mr. Freeman, and I'm sure they told you the story about how he locked himself in the john and couldn't get out. But, as I say, my memories are, you know, everything was in such a whirl and we were having at the library all of these air raid practices and what not.

Q: So you were pretty much engaged with your job.

Mrs. L.: Yeah. We, during the war, came to regret very much that we were the only Nimitzes in the telephone directory. This was bad, and we called the phone company about getting an unlisted phone, but at that time phones were at such a premium and an unlisted phone is a nuisance.

Q: Crackpots and...

Mrs. L.: Yeah, and they would say, "Well, we'll take the phone out," you know. They were willing to do that, but of course we weren't interested in that. But they would not give us an unlisted number. So we finally devised a code. We'd tell our friends, "Call up, let the phone ring once, and hang up immediately, and wait a minute and then dial again." And then we would answer the phone. Otherwise, you know, we didn't know what was going to...Actually, most of the messages were friendly, you know. I don't remember any really hostile ones. They all had good advice, you know.

Q: They didn't expect to get the Admiral on the phone, did they?

Mrs. L.: No, no, no. They just wanted us to convey their good ideas as to how to win the war. Of course, Dad got many letters like this, many of which he would send back to Nancy and me for us to enjoy. One darling one from a rabbi in New York started out, "My most beloved R. Ad.," and I forget what his advice was. Then there was another one that told him to cut out the island-hopping, to just sit on his anthill.

Q: Sit on - what was that?

Mrs. L.: Sit on his anthill - you just sit on your anthill.

Q: Well, he communicated with you frequently during the war?

Mrs. L.: Yes, he did. He really did. You know, maybe Navy public relations was not as much on the ball as Army public relations. They were always - you could always tell when some Army general was going to talk, but we very frequently missed the times when Dad appeared on the radio because the Navy never notified us, and we would sometimes be called halfway through a talk by friends who hoped we were listening, you know. But we heard - we had letters from him quite frequently. And then every time he came back to Washington for a conference, this was all very hush-hush, and we would be called up by the Navy and be told that his plane would be coming in at Anacostia at such-and-such a time, and a car would call for us and pick us up. It was always, it seemed to me in February or March, during a blizzard, and we'd all go down looking like something that had been turned up under a log, and this great big flying boat would come in and Dad and Spruance and all these people right out of the Pacific, tanned, you know, and they all looked wonderful. We always looked so gruesome at that time of the year.

Q: Well, then, would he stay with you?

Mrs. L.: Yeah, and -- oh, this was another thing. Nancy and I had a -- this was when I began to hate the press. We had a knockdown-dragout fight with them. It wasn't so much the reporters, it was these miserable feature writers, and there was one woman who made our lives particularly miserable. She decided that she was going to do an article on the Fleet Admiral's daughters who were working - actually working. And she was very obnoxious, and called us at home several times, and she usually got Nancy, who really was very brisk and said we had nothing to say and don't bother coming around because we wouldn't let her in. So, she, in her turn, got annoyed with us and said, well, the Public Library was a public place and we couldn't very well stop her from coming down there. Nancy said, no, that was right. So she came down one afternoon and Nancy was on duty at the information desk in the lobby, and she...

Q: She also worked at the Public Library?

Mrs. L.: Yeah. And Nancy wouldn't talk to her, so she sat and watched - well, she stood, I guess, there was no chair, but she stood and watched Nancy transact business with the public for about 45 minutes, and then she wanted to know where the music division was. I can still remember Nancy coming downstairs to the basement and saying, "Kate, this is Gwen Morgan. Don't tell her a thing." And Gwen Morgan then pulled up a chair and, because I wouldn't talk to her, she watched me transact business with the public. And then she wrote a surprisingly good-tempered article. Oh, you know, I guess she - because of Dad she couldn't very well say these two - well, you know. She turned up later on Nimitz Day, came up and was very gushy to Mother. Nancy and I just giggled like crazy. And the other person that we dealt with at that time was Dale Carnegie. Did you hear about that?

Q: No.

Mrs. L.: That was a holy mess. Here was the man who wrote this book on <u>How To Win Friends and Influence People</u>. We got a letter from him and he said - it started out like this, "You are doubtless familiar with my radio program "Little Known Facts about Well Known People." We weren't, actually, but we found out a lot later, and I propose to do one on your father. Kindly fill out the enclosed questionnaire and return it to me at your earliest convenience. I will be in Washington on April 6 and will call on you at the Public Library," you know, not is it convenient or anything. Well - and the questionnaire was about six pages long, and it was - this was the kind of thing, "Does your Mother have any intimate names for your father? What is your Father's favorite breakfast cereal?" that kind of, you know, and, well, after tearing the questionnaire in half, Nancy said, "I'll write him," and, you know, I was afraid to let her, so I said, no, I'll write him. I said, "Dear Mr. Carnegie, My Mother is in Berkeley. My Mother is the one to whom you should write for information about my Father." I didn't say anything about the 6th of April, and then he wrote back a very snippy letter and said that he would call on us at the Library, and so I went to my boss and said, you know, "This man is annoying us. How about a week's leave?" We had it coming to us anyway, and she said, fine. So Nancy and I just took off and went up to the Cape. Chester was on leave, too (Carnegie). And we never told him, and he arrived. I guess he was ready to kill us. But that's my memory of Dale Carnegie who wrote all these books on how to get along with people. Oh!

The other letter that we got that Nancy was going to answer - thank God I didn't let her do that - was from an admiral's wife who was very high up in the DAR, and this was just after the war started, and she said, "Dear Catherine and Nancy, I've been checking into your ancestry and I find that you are eligible to become members of the DAR." This was just after Marian Anderson and all these - Nancy said, "I'll answer that." And I said, "Oh, no, you won't."

Q: Nancy was the hatchet girl?

Mrs. L.: Oh! Yes, she had more aplomb about this than I did, but we both - but, oh, one day later I came back for a conference,

Gwen Morgan called us up, "Your Father's back," and Nancy said, yes. "Have you seen him?" And Nancy said, "Of course we've seen him. As a matter of fact, he had breakfast with us this morning." And she said, "Oh, tell me about it." And Nancy said, "Well, the Admiral wore white muslin with a pale blue sash." I think Gwen Morgan said, "Go to hell," but I'm not quite sure. She was absolutely at the end of her patience. But I still feel, you see, the interest that she was creating in us was purely artificial. I mean, you know, this was a matter of creating the interest and then satisfying it, and I didn't think this was legitimate. Neither did Nancy. I feel this way about the people who write about Mrs. Kennedy, too, you know. It's just a way to make a living.

Q: Will you talk a little about your Father's attitude toward the press?

Mrs. L.: I don't think he ever - I never heard him say anything, except about photographers. Oo, they used to burn him up, you know, "You stand over here, you stand over here, and you stand over here." He wasn't used to being pushed around. I think he had very good relations with the press and was always extremely tactful, or else his aides were, don't you Jay?

Capt. L.: Yes.

Mrs. L.: At the time we were married, Mother said, "Now, the Navy public relations will send a photographer to cover - we were married in a very small ceremony just before, this was in

Lay - 64

March of '45, and we had about 25 people there. Dad was back. They were - what were they planning, the Iwo Jima campaign, or...?

Capt. L.: He was going to commission a...

Mrs. L.: Daddy [Mary] was going to commission a destroyer on the 11th, and we found, interestingly enough, that the one thing you cannot fix in Washington no matter who you are or who you know, is the three-day wait between the time you announce your intentions - and they had a bad weather report - we were supposed to be married on the 9th of March, and Mary was christening this destroyer on the 11th in San Francisco, and they said it might not be good flying weather, and the chaplain said, don't worry, I'll marry them at one minute past midnight on Thursday - on Friday, one minute past midnight - and that will be all right. But Mother said to me, "Now, I know how you and Nancy feel about the press and you're going to be - get some calls the minute this announcement comes out, and please, for your Father's sake," you know. She knows both of us. "Please, for your Father's sake, be careful what you say." So the first thing that happened was on Thursday night, the night before the wedding, Jay and I were going out to dinner and about 4 in the afternoon The Times-Herald called and this woman said, "We're sending a car for you," you know, not is this convenient for you or - "We're sending a car for you and we'll pick you up and take you - we don't have a good decent [recent] photograph of you," just a photograph of me at the desk, you know, passing out books or something, "and we'll take you down to the office and take a picture." I said, "Oh, I'm sorry but no." And she said, "Oh, we'll be there." So I just said, "Well, I won't. I won't be there." Jay came about 6 o'clock - they hadn't come yet - and we knew we were going to have a little difficulty, so we just sat there very quietly. We decided we'd wait till they'd come and gone, and sure enough, we heard the elevator come up and bang, bang, bang at the door, and we just sat there on the sofa, didn't say a word, and finally when we were pretty sure that the coast was clear, we took the elevator down to the basement and went out the janitor's entrance. That was the night before the wedding, and then Friday afternoon, about two hours before the wedding, I got a call from Life magazine and at that time they were running a series, you remember, on the back page "Life Goes to This, Life Goes to That," and so this woman said, "This is Life magazine and we'd like to come and take pictures of the wedding." I was on firm ground here, and I said very politely "Well - I ~~one of our good old antique chairs in the dining room~~ I said, "Well, I'm sorry, but, no, we are not having any photographers. The Navy photographer will be there and he will give pictures to all the news media." She was very insistent and said, "Oh, but why do you feel so strongly about this?" So I said, "Well, I just feel this way. But anyway it's out of my hands." And so very ungraciously, you know,, concluded the telephone conversation, and about ten years later when we came back to Arlington we were invited to a dinner party. I have a real talent for putting my foot in it when I don't even try, and there were about ten people there, and this lady came up to me and she said, "You were Catherine Nimitz, weren't you?" And I said, "Yes." It was terrible, here she was leading with her chin and I said, "Yes, I was." And she said, "Do you remember the afternoon that you were married Life magazine called up and wanted to send a photographer to your wedding." And I could feel my hackles rise, and I said, "I certainly do." The hostess is right in between us, you know, "What's the matter?" And she said, "Well, I was the person who called. Would you like to tell me now why you felt that way?" And I said, "Oh, I'd be delighted. After all, you only get married once so if you can't have things the way you want to at your one wedding," and this - she was on her third husband and she must have thought I knew this - wow.

Q: Well, your Father - I've heard several officers say this - that he was very reticent about reporting some of the events in the Pacific at the time, although the press was clamoring for...

Mrs. L.: Well, he was. That's right. He was. I think he and Drew Pearson had a couple of arguments. (TO JTL) I think that you said your skipper did, too. I mean, people felt that the press really was...

Capt. L.: Well, a lot of it still had a military value. You didn't want the enemy to know what you were up to at that time, and particularly on the amphibious operations, because, you see, it really didn't matter with us, you know, because we'd not send the messages off immediately, we'd hold up until after we made the landing, for instance, before we let them go. You didn't want to tip your hand ahead of time.

Q: One incident that I heard - I was, I guess it was the Battle of Midway, which Admiral Nimitz did not want to have get to the press immediately, but the Air Force apparently was quite gleeful and I believe the first press coverage assigned the credit to the Air Force, you see, for having accomplished this great battle. And this was very discouraging to some of the staff officers around the Admiral, but he was adamant about it.

Mrs. L.: I never heard him comment on this, but I do know that he was reticent about the press, but I think that his relations were - his personal relations with them - were cordial. I never read anything at all - Robert Rouark came the nearest to saying anything even faintly disparaging, and this was way after the war, when there was some talk that Truman might ask Dad to do something. I forget what it was. And Rouark, commenting on this, said, "Oh, he's all right, but he's an old man and he's tired." And I thought, "nuts to you, Rouark." I couldn't stand his writing anyway. And that certainly was not an unfriendly comment. That was simply an honest expression of his opinion. But I never heard of any unpleasantness.

Q: Well, I think it was more the tradition of the Navy, wasn't it? I mean the Navy are always reticent about public relations...

Mrs. L.: Who was it that spilled the beans about the Japanese code? That was a Chicago paper, wasn't it? I mean, after all!

Capt. L.: All these things cost us. Well, the submarines, for instance, when somebody spilled the beans about the Japs dropping the depth charges too shallow.

Mrs. L.: Oh, they said, Uhm.

Capt. L.: Now we know.

Mrs. L.: One lovely headline - I think this was during the war - referred to Dad and had a beautiful typo, as the Navy's two-headed admiral. We gave him a terribly rough time about that in the bosom of the family - instead of tow-headed.

Q: Did he take ribbing well?

Mrs. L.: Oh, marvellously. You see we sat around - nobody got away with anything. I think that's the way a family should be. Nobody gets away with anything in this family when the kids are home. You know, he really could be peeved, and he - the people on the Riegal [Risel], the orderlies, used to ~~say used to~~ hang around and listen to the family at dinner because, they said, "He's very strict, but those kids can get away with murder." Well, we were never disrespectful. He wouldn't have put up with that. But we certainly had an awful lot of - he used to have a couple of standard lectures when we were growing up. One was directed mainly at Chester, "At Annapolis, you won't be able to - or at Annapolis, you will have to.." And the other one started out, "Haven't you children any respect for your parents?" and it got to the point here, you know, he would come out with one of these or the other, and we could always tell when he was about to give us a little lecture. On one occasion, at the table, he opened his mouth and either Chester or I - and I really don't remember which one of us it was - said, "What's it going to be this time?" He said, "What do you mean?" This person said, "At Annapolis" or "Haven't you children any respect for your parents?" Mother just cracked up, and I will say for Dad that he cracked up too. You don't realize until one of your kids picks you up sometimes, you know...

Q: What kind of punishment did he indulge in when he did?

Mrs. L.: I'd say when we were little we got spanked occasionally, but it was more deprivation of privileges, I guess. He was much easier to get around than Mother, and this was funny because we were on a strict allowance, and Mother being a New Englander thought that we should, you know, have a great respect for the value of money and if we got behind or got in a bind, we could always cadge a little from Dad. And after Nancy and I started to work for the District of Columbia Library - you know the government of the District of Columbia is run like a Gilbert and Sullivan operetta, it's just awful - and they were always putting riders on the budget, you know, and so we would suddenly find ourselves with no pay checks. While we were living at home, this was fine for us, but it was really rough on the kids who were from outside the city. But we would go home and say, "Dad, can you lend us $10 or, you know, we didn't get paid," and of course he'd always give us the money and then when we came round to pay him back, he'd wave us off impatiently and say, "Give it to Mother. I don't want it," and we'd go to give it to Mother and she'd say, "Oh, give it to your Father. I don't want it." I guess they figured, having instilled it into us, that it was safe to let it go by the boards.

Q: Your brother told me that - maybe this pertained only to him as the male member of the family and a future naval officer - he said your Father seemed to apply the same kind of rule he applied to men on board ship. He expected his children to measure up to certain circumstances, and this was an unspoken thing, often. He just expected it and you fulfilled his expectations.

Mrs. L.: Did Chet make the comment that he made, you know, when he sold his first and only short story to a magazine, the first time he ever submitted one, and they asked him for a biographical sketch and he said...

Q: He didn't tell me that he wrote a short story.

Mrs. L.: Well - he - Chester is very creative. Not only very musical but has a real talent for writing and while he was in Coronado he enrolled in a short story course - a writing course at night - and wrote for the class, and then when he - I think his next duty - we were all at Norfolk together, and he submitted a story to - I think he sent it to Argosy - but it's part of a syndicate, and they bought it for <u>Adventure</u> magazine, and I think he got $200 for it. He was thrilled to death. But they asked him to supply an autobiographical note. He submitted it under a pen name because he felt that the Navy wasn't enthusiastic about having their people writing, and the autobiographical note said that the author of this story was the son of a naval officer who, when he was born, aimed him at the Naval Academy and pulled the trigger and this man said "I was 20 before I found out there were any other colleges." And I think this is absolutely true. I don't think Chet really wanted to go anywhere else, but, as he said, he never heard about any other college because Dad had had such a wonderful experience there that that was the best thing he could envision for Chet, and was just...

Q: And your Mother likewise.

Mrs. L.: Yes. There was just no question but what he was going to the Naval Academy. Chester's never done any more writing. I guess he hasn't had any time since.

Q: I don't see how he has.

Mrs. L.: But he was so tickled. Joan was out the day he got the acceptance, and he called me up. He had come home from lunch - he was at the Staff College - and he called me up and he said, "Kate, Kate, guess what!" He read me the letter and he said, "What I like is "I admire your story, I would like to buy it for <u>Adventure</u> magazine."" I think, maybe, when he retires he might go back to writing.

Q: I should think that would have spurred him on to do something else.

Mrs. L.: I guess. I would think so, too. But I think he can. I think he might later on.

Q: During the war, when your father communicated with you, did he ever comment on his own experiences?

Mrs. L.: No. Well, everything was so sort of hush-hush, you know. Oh, one rather funny thing, he did bring us some macadamia nuts one time when he came back, and he said he was absolutely on Mrs. MacArthur's black list because he had sent some to the MacArthur boy who had gotten violently sick on them. They are very dangerous, you know.

Q: Well, what did he write about?

Mrs. L.: Oh - well, I have a couple of letters here. One that he wrote, it was really a lovely letter that he wrote when he was just going over to sign the surrender and I think he probably wrote to each one of us children so that we'd have a letter on the...

Q: I was certainly delighted that was one letter your Mother saved.

Mrs. L.: What? The one...

Q: He wrote immediately after signing.

Mrs. L.: Yeah. This is a very nice letter. "Dear Catherine,

Today (this was dated 1 September 45) in the pelting rain and rough water, I boarded a destroyer in Lower Tokyo Bay and went to Yokohama to call on the Supreme Commander of the Allied Powers - SCAP, for short - General MacArthur at his quarters in the New Grand Hotel in Yokohama. His headquarters are in the Customshouse Building. Yokohama is like a dead city with very little activity. There are Japanese police and gendarmes on duty at SCAP quarters, and they act as if we were not in sight. They are not sullen or amazed, as one might expect. They simply do not see us. So far, the occupation has gone ahead with no violence or signs of it. When Junior arrives tomorrow his gang will walk ashore as they would in San Francisco, but without the welcome they would receive in San Francisco. The Allied POWs in the Japanese camps are the only ones who delightedly welcome us to Japan. I understand that there are some 38,000, including civilians, of which number about 8,000 are American. After leaving SCAP about noon today, we boarded a naval hospital ship Benevolence in the Bay, where some 450 ex-POWs were recovering from their bad treatment, and they were badly treated, too, beating, starvation rations, solitary confinement, and so forth. They will be sent home as rapidly as their condition and transportation permits. Tomorrow is the big day, and 9 a.m. is the hour when the Japanese emissaries sign the formal terms of surrender. I suspect there will be a rash of suicides after that. You should see the ships in the Bay, hundreds of ms U.S. with a few British ships. We have a huge fleet outside ready to fly in planes if necessary. In a few minutes I will go to call on

Admiral Fraser, R.N. on the <u>Duke of York</u> anchored close by, partly on official business, partly because I like him, and mostly to get a Scotch and soda before dinner because our ships are dry. It may be a day or so before I can join you so I'm sending you this in the mail now, hoping it finds you well and happy. Worlds of love to you and Nancy from your Dad.
P.S. Hope you save some of the bourbon for VJ Day."

Q: Save some of the bourbon for VJ Day?

Mrs. L.: He had apparently sent us a bottle of bourbon. And then I've also kept the letter that he wrote me on - this is dated the 4th of April. I won't read it all but this was after I had gone back to work...

Q: What year?

Mrs. L.: '45. See, we were married on the 9th of March, and this was just to say that he enjoyed hearing about my meeting all my new relatives in Missouri and "I now give you written assurance of our - Mother and me - high regard and great esteem for our son-in-law. You could not have picked anyone we could like more than Junior and I predict for you two a long and wonderful life just as Mother's and mine have been and will continue to be until death do us part." Then he goes on and says some very nice things about my friend over here..."

Capt. L.: That was in confidence!

Mrs. L.: Yes. Interesting   he says, "This war in the Pacific can't last for ever and there is hope we can conclude it by the end of 1946." You see, this was written on 12 April 45. "If not sooner, and then we can all be more normal again. The European situation seems to be in hand and our Japanese war is going along as well as can be expected at present. By the time the large air reinforcements come from the European theater, we expect to have land areas and fields ready so they can go to work on the Japs at once. In the meantime, we are not idle. I hope you are completely recovered from the sore throat. With worlds of love to you and Junior, I remain, your devoted Dad."

I would say Nancy and I heard from him every couple of weeks.

Q: And, apparently, your Mother every day.

Mrs. L.: Oh, yes. This was really good concern, though, to...

Q: And he got to see her quite frequently, didn't he, when he came over?

Mrs. L.: Yes. Yes, he did, and I guess she also didn't know until the last minute, and I'm sure she told you of the time that the plane hit this submerged log and they all walked ashore, sloshing. I have an absolute phobia about flying. I used to hate it when he'd fly into Washington. A couple of times we had an ice storm the night before and they'd divert the plane to Jacksonville, Florida, and Nancy and I would lie awake waiting for the phone to ring at 2 in the morning. I'd rather walk than fly. I think it's not here to stay, the plane.

Q: Tell me about his coming back from the Pacific and becoming

CNO.

Mrs. L.: Well, my memories of that are mostly about that Gothic house that they lived in up on Observatory Hill, and Mary, at that time, was the only child living at home. I think she had a very thin time because the family were really out or entertaining all the time and...

Q: Heavy social duties.

Mrs. L.: Yeah, and Mother would call up and say, "Don't you and Jay want to come in and have dinner at the Observatory," it would be summer time and very hot...

Q: Where were you living then?

Mrs. L.: Living out in Maryland. And I'd say, "Ooh, put on clothes and come into town? No." And she'd say, "But Mary is going to be here all alone in that dining room. It's the fourth time this week." And I'd say, "Send her out and we'll feed her out here, but we don't want to come in." We were expecting our first child that July and it was one of the hottest summers on record, and we weren't particularly thrilled with the idea of getting dressed up, as you'd have to do to go down to the Observatory. So Mary would very often come out and have dinner with us. While he was at the Observatory, he was getting all these postwar decorations from the various embassies and legations around town, and Jay and I got in the mail one day a formal invitation to a ceremony at the Greek - I guess it's a legation - where Dad was going to be awarded the

Cross of St. George, I think it was their highest military decoration, and the invitation was for July 31st, and I called up Mother and said, "What will I do?" This was the day that I was due to go to the hospital and have Jimmy, and I said, "I know enough to send formal regrets, but obviously we received this invitation because they knew we're daughter and son-in-law and we're living right here. What are they going to think? They're going to be insulted." It was a real dilemma. And so Mother said, after thinking it over, she said, "Well, I would send the formal regret today and then tomorrow call the Legation and explain to the secretary who you are and why you sent the regrets." So I wrote the formal regrets and the next day I 'phoned, thinking I might get somebody who spoke heavily accented English. Instead I got somebody I could picture chewing gum and I said, "This is Mrs. James Lay, and I sent a regret and I want to explain why. My father and so forth." But I said, "That is the date that I am due to go to the hospital to have our first baby." There was silence for a minute, and then she said, "Oh, honey, that's a shame. I knew I should have gotten those invitations out earlier." Isn't that unbelievable?

Q: She connected, didn't she?

Mrs. L.: Jay thought it over and said, "Yeah, last October would have been a good time."

Q: In that time he had to spend a lot of hours on the Hill, didn't he?

Mrs. L.: Yes, he did. And we did go to a few parties at the House and met -- I remember meeting the Eisenhowers there one night. They had - their parties always started out rather formally, but they are not formal people at all, and they had a ping pong table in the downstairs - in the main lobby - and it always ended up with - well, the women guests would go up and borrow, maybe in their formals, go up and borrow clothes from Mother and get on their short skirts and come down and they'd have ping pong matches. And it always turned out to be very...

Q: That dispersed the cobwebs, didn't it?

Mrs. L.: Yes, it did.

Q: Tell me, your Father was a great story teller...

Mrs. L.: He certainly was.

Q: at dinner parties. Can you tell me some of those stories?

Mrs. L.: I'm sure Mother and Nancy have told you.

Q: Well, they told me some.

Mrs. L.: But Mother spent an awful lot of her time rolling her eyes, trying to catch his eye, you know, so that he wouldn't. I can't...

Q: I've been trying to make a collection of them and I've succeeded to some extent, but most people can't remember them.

Mrs. L.: No. I really don't know. What have you got in your

collection?

Q: Well, you start enumerating some that you remember.

Mrs. L.: Well, I'm sure you've got the midwife story...

Q: Yes, I have. I had that from Nancy.

Mrs. L.: Chester used to say, "Just tell it one more time, Dad. I want to get it for technique." I don't know where he heard that. But I can't think, really. He was always telling stories, and they were always funny...

Q: He always had new ones.

Mrs. L.: Yeah. People just kept him supplied. His aide, LaMar, told me that during the war it got to the point people would come out with really gross - the word got around that he liked stories, and he really had enough taste so that he was not interested in anything that was   or just plain, as the boys say now, gross. His stories, I always thought, were pretty funny. I think between Nancy and Mother - I can't think of any. The midwife one comes to mind immediately, but that's all.

Q: That's perhaps the most famous of all.

Mrs. L.: Yeah. Every once in a while I think of one at school and I come out with it in the teachers' room, but I haven't thought of any recently. Jay, you served on the Augusta with him, you ought to remember.

Capt. L.: He didn't usually tell them on the bridge.

Mrs. L.: Not on the bridge, no.

Q: Or during inspections! Or for the benefit, really, of junior officers!

Mrs. L.: He had an awful lot of cute anecdotes that he - of his own experiences.

Q: Was he particularly happy in Washington at that time? I mean, did he really like to be CNO, or did he...?

Mrs. L.: I think he honestly wanted to be CNO. I mean, I think that he, you know, I'm sure Mother - you must know that there was some question as to whether he would be or not, and I think he really felt that he wanted - I think he wanted to be CNO. He did not want, you know, to succeed himself...

Q: You mean for a second term?

Mrs. L.: Yeah.

Q: But this was the ultimate!

Mrs. L.: It's hard for me to say, but I do think - I mean, there was some question as to whether - I think it was...

Q: Wasn't that bound up in Forrestal and his preference?

Mrs. L.: I believe so, since you mention it. Yes, I believe it was. And I think he would have been quite perturbed if he hadn't had the opportunity. I wouldn't think he particularly enjoyed the job very much, though.

Q: Well, that's just what I'm wondering about. I don't have

any evidence on it, but I wonder if he was particularly happy...

Mrs. L.: I don't think so.

Q: After having been...

Mrs. L.: Actually, he'd always rather be at sea than anywhere else.

Q: Exactly. A man of that action, and this was a kind of demobilization of the Navy.

Mrs. L.: Yes. Yes, I think so.

Q: Yes, this was presiding over - the disintegration of the war machine that he had commanded.

Mrs. L.: Yes. I think that's right.

Q: Were you present when he said farewell to Washington?

Mrs. L.: No. I think Jay and I had already gone out to - that was in '48, wasn't it?

Q: Yes.

Mrs. L.: Jay had the Orlick [Orleck] on the West Coast - a destroyer - and we had gone to San Diego. Then Dad came out to be Navy Day speaker in October of '47 - I guess it was, because the twins were born in '48 - and I saw him then. He was still officially on active duty, and then shortly after that he retired - I mean, he didn't retire, but he was stepped down from being CNO, and he and Mother came out to San Diego. By this time we knew that Jay was going to WesPac, the crafty character. I was going to have twins. He was going three weeks before the twins were due and not come back till they were eight months old. That's planning. And Mother and Dad were going to stay with me until the twins were born until, oh, I got somebody to help me, and then they were going up to Berkeley and look for a place, you know, a house to buy, which they did. I guess they went up around April of '48. They stayed in San Diego until about April. Some very funny things happened in connection with the twins. That was another time when I came to loathe and detest the press, and I wrote Jay. I said, "You don't even get a byline. These are the Admiral's twins. They had to mention my name, but they don't mention your name at all." And he used to get all of this fan mail, you know, quantities of it, and at this point he and Mother, although they were staying with me, would go off on these one-night speaking tours and, you know, be gone two or three days and Dad used to/say open all the mail. About that time a magazine article by Admiral Halsey appeared in the Saturday Evening Post - that famous one where he said he didn't give a dam for any fighting man who didn't drink or smoke - Dad - it was one of the few times I ever saw him really riled by his mail. He usually thought it was funny, even when he got it, you know, from nuts, and this one said, "Dear Admiral, I've always admired you very much, but I am very much disappointed in you. I have just finished reading an article in the Saturday Evening Post in which you said that you did not give a (and then she wrote "dime") BECAUSE SHE WAS TOO VIRTUOUS TO USE THE WORD) for any fighting man who didn't drink or smoke, and I've seen your picture with those darling little twins," oh, and, you know, the idea of being - you're supposed to be a good influence. Well that really got him, and he sat down and wrote a biting answer, sarcastic answer, saying, "Dear Madam, You've obviously confused me with another naval personage (he didn't mention Halsey by name). I did not write the article, and I am sure that a woman of your obvious rectitude would wish to correct the mistaken impression." Then he and Mother went off on a speaking engagement, and about a week later came this thick, thick letter from this woman, and I said to myself, "This is going to be good. She's going to grovel for ten pages." I opened it. No letter at all, but out fell a tract, "Steps to Christ, Army and Navy Edition." By that time we all thought it was funny.

If you turn off the tape recorder, I'll tell you the funniest story of all, but I won't tell it for...

Q: The story of the aide who turned out to need aid himself?

Mrs. Um. I felt so sorry for him. I don't think he'd ever been an aide to anybody, and he was simply told off to...

Q: This happened when?

Mrs. L.: I think this was at the time of Admiral Halsey's funeral, and it was frightfully hot and, as I say, Dad just cannot take hot weather - or couldn't take hot weather - and he had been out on the Coast and wasn't used to the Washington summer. We were living in Arlington. They not only assigned him an aide that had never been an aide, but they assigned him a driver who didn't know his way around Washington, couldn't find the River Entrance to the Pentagon and that sort of thing. And the morning - it may have been the night before the funeral, and the morning of the funeral he had the driver take him over to the Pentagon for something, and they got lost and wound all around, and barely got back to the house in time to change into whites for the service which was going to be in Washington Cathedral. I had three kids, little kids, playing out in the yard and Dad and the aide came in, "We don't have any time for lunch. Never mind. I have to get dressed," and Dad went into the guest room to get dressed and the aide asked if he could change in the living room, and I said, "Fine," and the aide was already uncomfortably aware that he was weighed in the balance and found wanting, and, firstly, Dad came out hot and bothered and he said, "Get me a pair of Junior's white uniform socks." He'd unrolled the ones he brought and there was a great big fat hole in the heel, and I said, "Oh, gosh, Junior hasn't worn white uniform socks for ages," and I had to go up in the attic, go up a ladder, this small space, and the temperature must have been 104, and I was dying, and there was no time to waste, and I finally managed to find a rather yellowed pair of Junior's white uniform socks and brought them down. Meanwhile, the aide came out and said to me piteously, "Look, have you got a safetypin?" (The snap on the high collar of his uniform.) I want you to know that he had skivvies on the lamp, on the piano. He was absolutely in a dither, and I got a safetypin and I was trying to pin this.

And you know it's starched and impossible to get a pin through it, and Dad came and stood in the doorway and said, "What are you doing?" And the aide said, and I said at the same time, "Trying to put a safety pin..." Dad said, "There's no time for that. Nobody's going to be looking at you, anyway. Come on." So they went off to the funeral...

Q: Without the safetypin?

Mrs. L.: Yeah, without the safetypin. Actually, I don't remember whether I managed to get it together or not, but we were all just streaming with perspiration. And they finally got back about, oh, in the middle of the afternoon, and Dad said, "I'm going to take a shower," he walked in and the aide just looked as though, you know, he'd had it, and I said, "How about a cold beer?" and he said, "I'd love one." At that point Dad came out in his bathrobe. He'd started to get into the shower and he thought of the aide and he said, "Are you married?" And the aide said, "Yes, Sir," and Dad said, "Your wife should have checked your uniform." And that was just too much for me and I turned to him and I said, "You're married, why didn't your wife check your socks?" I felt so sorry for him. Oh, poor man. I must admit when Dad got cooled off and had a beer, he was his usual affable self. I don't remember that man's name, but I guess he regards this as one of the darkest days of his life. You know, Dad was a little bit hard of hearing and I was awfully happy he didn't hear - they came East for the fiftieth...

Q: When did that come on him?

Mrs. L.: Er, oh, I think he's always been a little...

Capt. L.: Even when he had the <u>Augusta</u>.

Mrs. L.: Yes, in fact, he was quoted in the ship's paper as saying, "What, what's that," that was supposed to be his favorite. He always denied this, you know. He just said people muttered, didn't speak up distinctly. But I think it was much worse after the war, because of the guns, you know, but he and Mother came East to go - it would have been in '55 - to go to their 50th anniversary homecoming at the Naval Academy. This was a funny story. The CNO gave him a car and a driver. Jay and I were going down with them to our 24th, and we had for us working a very erratic, fat, colored girl who as Dad - we were all dressed to the nines and about to leave the house, and Dad came out and she said to him, "Doll Baby, you sure do look sexy." He didn't hear it. Mother and Junior and I all...

Q: And he didn't hear it?

Mrs. L.: Oh, we told him afterwards. Yes, he thought it was funny. We got down to Annapolis, and of course there were - it was a rather small group from the class of 1905, and so what they do, as you know, is gather up any widows of adjacent classes, anybody - you know there's always provision made - nobody is left sitting, you know, alone. And, well, we didn't see each other all evening and - because we were widely separated - at the conclusion we met back at the car, and the Marine driver, he must have had a terrible time. He was shaking all the way home, he was laughing so hard. Dad got in and he said to Mother, "We'll skip the 75th and I'll take you to the 100th." Mother was laughing and, he said, "Oh, oh, those women, those women." It developed that as they got ready to sit down, it was a round table, Dad always the genial host, said, "Now wait a minute. No man shall sit beside his wife." And there were fewer men than women, but they divided them up and he found himself between two ladies whose names fortunately I don't remember, who apparently really gave him the business. One of them wanted to get some kind of legislation through Congress about something. Roberta McCain, you know, Jack's wife, said afterwards when I told her who they were, "Oh, God, if he ever sinned in his life, he's paid for it." And Mother kept laughing and saying, "Well, darling, you could have had me, but you had to go out and be - you know" This Marine who was driving really was just - Junior was sitting in front with him - or was Dad sitting in front with him? I don't remember, but I could see him, he was in hysterics. I think those homecomings are kind of gruesome, myself. We went to our 35th. All that smoke and those parties, paper cups, The young midshipmen seeing the older ones that way, I think is very bad.

Q: The President of his class - 1905 - was in Annapolis now.

Mrs. L.: Who is that?

Q: Captain Court.

Mrs. L.: Oh, there's a photograph of him in the class - I

think he was at the class luncheon that Dad had. Did you know that Admiral Furlong remarried? He was a classmate of Dad's.

Q: Oh, really! Was he?

Mrs. L.: Yes Dutch Furlong and this — he's in his 80s. Mother was so happy about this, she — Admiral Furlong's wife has been dead for some time, and Mother called up not too long ago and said, "You'll never know who's just got married. I had a wedding invitation." There aren't too many of the class left. I found some wonderful pictures — most of the pictures and the letters and things, I think are duplicates of what everybody in the family has — but while I was going through the boxes the other day, I found — have you seen the one "The Burial of Skinny & Steam of 1905." My father is in a most undignified pose, I'm sure. If it weren't for the fact that I know they couldn't get anything to drink, I would think they were all soused. Isn't that lovely?

Q: Certainly is some picture.

Mrs. L.: And this I brought down because I don't know any of the people in it except Dad, but if you want to know how he reacted to children ~~in the Navy~~, he was at some school — I think in the Bay area or one of the Nimitz schools and they took a picture of him with the children. ~~Miss Orville Cox at the same party.~~

Q: I've seen...

Mrs. L. Really, the only classmates that I remember very vividly are Bruce Canega, whom I just loved and Admiral Furlong. The others are just names to me

Capt. L.: G. O. Carter-

Mrs. L.: Oh yes, G.O. Carter, I met briefly. He was darling, but we just met him that one time. He and Dad were both on the crew together.

Q: I have a copy of that picture. That's a beautiful picture.

Mrs. L.: I just love it.

Q: Dedication of a school.

Mrs. L.: The other day a little girl came in for a library card, and was getting the transient, which goes on all the time, you know, this being a Navy community, and she said, "By the way,, my teacher told me to be sure and come up and tell you that my last school was a Nimitz school." And I said, "Where was this?" And she said, "Honolulu." And she said, "You know that we have a birthday party on your father's birthday every year, and every room has a cake and ice cream." I said, "He'd be very pleased to know this."

Q: Do you have any recollections of his assignment to the United Nations?

Mrs. L.: Yeah. I know that my Mother was particularly delighted because, she said that ever since she'd been a child she had dreamed of going to see the Vale of Kashmir. It always seemed to be, you know, to represent to her the epitome of the romantic, you know, and they spent that summer of - what - '51, I guess it would have been, or maybe - being briefed at the UN. I can't remember what year it was. We were in Norfolk. Being briefed at the UN, and they really enjoyed meeting all of the people, the different nationalities at the UN, and my Mother had one very telling anecdote, I think. There were an awful lot of Long Island socialites that they met and went to parties with, and she talked about being at a luncheon in the delegates' dining room at the UN and seated next to her was a Long Island man - I don't know, I don't remember his name, really - and he looked around, and here were all these people of different hues and costumes, and he said to my Mother, "Do they allow foreigners to eat in here?" And Mother looked at him and said, "There are no foreigners at the UN." And he said, "I guess that's right." I think it was really a great disappointment when Dad finally decided that he could do nothing. They weren't going to stop shooting long enough, and he and Mother came down to Norfolk, and while they were staying with us, he said, "Would you do a little typing for me?" And I said innocently, "Why, I'd be delighted." And he handed me his official resignation from the UN, from that plebescite, and he said, "I would like an original and five copies." But, in typing it, it was the first time that I understood that this was a religious difference that was never going to be settled. He really didn't think that it would ever, you know, be amicably resolved, and there again he really - he was so explicit and so concise, but I remember typing it because I burned up the dinner while I was sitting up there typing, you remember? We had to eat the leftover chile from the night before.

Q: That must have been a real disappointment to him, because he actually prepared for this.

Mrs. L.: Yes. But you know afterwards they assassinated the Liaquat Ali and they assassinated somebody else. I think they would have, you know, gone for Dad too. I mean, I think there was a good chance that he would have been, you know.

Q: It's too bad that they didn't give him another assignment of some sort that would appear to be...

Capt. L.: I doubt that he would have taken it.

Mrs. L.: I doubt it, too. Actually he had many offers of university jobs, and of course many offers of business jobs. I don't think Mother was so enthusiastic about the business jobs, but I think she felt that he made a mistake not to do something, you know, not to have...

Q: What universities did he have...?

Mrs. L.: Oh, I can't remember. Well, of course, he was a Regent of the University of California, and he could have had - I think he had offers from other universities, I really don't remember now, but and then he did not want to succeed himself as a regent because he felt that this was ill-advised.

Q: Well, he still had tremendous energy and enthusiasm -

Mrs. L.: Oh, yeah.

Q: -- and it does seem that it was somewhat wasted.

Mrs. L.: Yes, I agree. Particularly as he really did not have anything but the Navy. That was his be-all and end-all. He enjoyed, you know, meeting other Navy people and people from all over the world came to see him in Berkeley. But he didn't have any what I would call avocation or a really hobby, other than his walking and...

Q: Could he not have a business...?

Mrs. L.: I don't think he would have been the least bit tempted. I do think he was asked to serve on various -- what do you call it?

Q: Boards?

Mrs. L.: Yes.

Q: So many, almost invariably, retired military people, naval people, have taken such assignments.

Mrs. L.: You know where Chet gets his terrific business acumen is from my Mother, who, even now, you know, has a lovely time fooling around with her stocks, and Chester gets a big kick out of it. Every time he goes out there she's got all these things to show him and tell him about, and he thinks she's got quite a flair. Dad really didn't, particularly. He had no interest.

Q: Tell me about his great love of children. How it was manifested?

Mrs. L.: Well, one way that it was manifested is that we were always welcome to bring people home, and on many, many Saturdays, I remember, particularly when we were in Berkeley, he'd organize a long walk in the Berkeley hills and encourage us to bring people along. Mother has a lot of snapshots, or had, of various groups of kids, and, you know, give him a watermelon and a deck of cards and a bunch of kids, and he was in seventh Heaven. He loved to do card tricks. He loved watermelon. He'd come in to us and if we'd get a watermelon, he'd get all the kids in the neighborhood in and carve us this watermelon and do card tricks for them. One time when we were in Berkeley, Mother and Nancy went up in the country and stayed for, I think, about six weeks. Nancy was thought to have a spot on her lung or something, and the doctor thought she ought to get out of the Berkeley climate, and Dad and Chester and I kept house. Well, Dad was an excellent cook, by the way. He was really very competent in the kitchen and very neat, very insistent that you clean up as you go along. And even during this time, you know, we'd come home and say, "Can so-and-so stay for dinner," or "Can I have so-and-so over?" It was perfectly fine. So, the more the merrier. He was marvellous with the twins and with Chet's children, I mean to the point where he could still change diapers, and he loved them, entertaining them, and I remember being frantic when I'd take them out to the store, because when they got to the point where they could walk, or crawl, they'd get out and one would make for the middle of Orange Avenue and the other would make for the fruit and the vegetables and start tossing them around.

I never knew which one to chase first, and Dad said, "That's very simple." He tied the inside shoe lace of each shoe together around the middle of the stroller so they couldn't get out. I'd never thought of this simple thing.

Q: In his latter days, did he attempt to read to children, as he did when you were...

Mrs. L.: Oh, yes. He read, and also played innumerable games of Scrabble with them, told them stories. I think he was always happy with young people around.

Q: What did he tell them? Sea stories and...?

Mrs. L.: About his experiences in the war. When we were in Norfolk, the teachers who lived next door asked Dad if he would come up and speak to the Larchmont Elementary School. I remember, Jimmy, until this time - you know, we had always played down his famous grandfather, this was just grandfather, you know, because we figured this would happen soon enough, and Dad came up in his Fleet Admiral's uniform and talked - and this is one of the few times that I actually heard him talk. I went and sat in the front row. And after he had finished talking, the kids were allowed to send up questions on 3 x 5s and he would read the question, and answer. And one of the questions, I remember, was, "How did you feel when you found that you were the commander-in-chief?" And he said, "Lonely," and then went on to say, you know, "It's all on you," and that a person in that position is bound to be lonely even though you have wonderful people to help you. The kids were quite enthusiastic, and Jimmy was insufferable after that. He had no stature at all in that school until - I mean, no unusual, but the minute this was over, he then, you know...

Q: He was a problem?

Mrs. L.: Yes. YES. They got over it, though, I mean when they were smart enough to realize. We have a wonderful picture of Jim taken when he was in the ROTC at Rogers High School and Dad was here visiting. I was really tempted to send it to Life magazine as "the highest and the lowest." Dad had his uniform on and Jim just as proud as punch in this terrible World War I castoff with all this junk jewelry, you know, and about 50 lbs overweight. Wonderful picture. And I never quite had the nerve to do it, because I figured, you know, you hate the press, this is violating their privacy, they wouldn't appreciate - Jimmy might have had a miserable time at school, too.

Q: Your Father apparently had a marvelous knack of surrounding himself with very capable men.

Mrs. L.: I guess he did.

Capt. L.: He was a very good judge of character.

Mrs. L.: I don't know. He didn't warn me about you.

Capt. L.: He should have.

Mrs. L.: Did you talk to any of the other Augusta sailors?

Q: Leverton.

Mrs. L.: Oh, yes.

Q: Moncure.

Mrs. L.: Leverton - the other twins.

Q: Yes, and your Father had a very great liking for them, too.

Mrs. L.: Oh, he loved them, absolutely loved them. I don't know how you could help it.

Capt. L.: I never will forget Bill Leverton telling me one time when I was in Washington, I asked him if he'd be glad when the kids were old enough not to believe in Santa Claus. He said, "I will not. They're happy with what they get now."

Q: A charming man, he is.

Mrs. L.: Oh, absolutely. Funny.

Capt. L.: He was the best man at our wedding.

Q: The one I know best is Waters, because he's on our Board and I see him quite frequently.

Mrs. L.: I don't know him very well. I think the last time I saw them was when we were in Virginia Beach.

Q: He's the oceanographer of the Navy.

Mrs. L.: And they're cousins of the Levertons, aren't they? She, Mrs. Waters - Muffie, is that her name? Sue - is a cousin of

Helen's.

Capt. L.: Mrs. Leverton and Mrs. Waters are first cousins.

Mrs. L.: Yes, and actually I think Helen and Bill met at the wedding when Helen was maid of honor, or Bill was best man, I don't remember, but, I mean, they met at that wedding. What's Sam Moncure doing now? Is he just...?

Q: He's vice president of the - I guess it's the Virginia Bank. It's a new bank. It's a combination of two that amalgamated in Alexandria.

Mrs. L.: He had a lovely sister who was married to a missionary that - and they were stationed in Suchow, and when we were on the - Dad was on the Augusta, we went out and spent a day at their house, had a trip on the canal. They had what looked like a typical Virginia colonial house out in the wilds of Suchow. They were a lovely couple. I don't know whatever happened to them. Haven't heard of them for years.

Q: His name is Cox.

Mrs. L.: Cox, right.

Q: And they live in Alexandria.

Mrs. L.: Oh, do they?

Q: Yes.

Mrs. L.: She looked enough like Sam to be a twin at the time that I remember her.

Q: Tell me about those days in China, when the family was out there.

Mrs. L.: Well, I didn't go out. They went out in November of '33 and I was a senior at the university, so I stayed and graduated and came out on the President Johnson and, as I say, the Augusta was at Kobe at the time that we put in there and I went to Shanghai almost immediately. Mother and Nancy and Mary and I went over to Japan. The temperature in Shanghai gets up to about 105. It's like Washington, only, you know, hotter. So we went over and spent the summer in Unzen, and then when I came back to Shanghai my New England Mother said, you know, "You're not going to sit around here and do nothing like some of these other girls," you know, "an idle mind is the devil's workshop" and all this, "You go to business school." So they found - this is fantastic - Farmers' Commercial College for Young Ladies run by a lovely pair of Australian cockneys on Pekin Road...

Q: In Shanghai?

Mrs. L. In Shanghai. And Nancy Jennings, whose father was a paymaster captain, and I were the only two American girls at the school. There was a large group of Eurasians, some Finnish girls, and we studied typing, shorthand, cable coding, the Chinese system of weights and measures, and all this business, and the man who ran it had been a court reporter. He was very much overweight and very florid complexion, and when he would start to dictate to us, you know, we found his dictation increasingly difficult to understand as the class went on. He had a great big enamel pitcher on the desk which he'd pour this tea, take a big drink, and one time, during the break, Nancy Jennings went up and it was almost straight rum. We went to school from 9 to 12, and then we had two hours off for tiffin, you know, as they do in Shanghai. We actually made the long trip home on the bus and then came back, and had an hour or so in the afternoon. I found this life completely incomprehensible, I mean, nothing happens in Shanghai until 5 o'clock, then they start having these teas, you know, which means bread and jam and crumpets and all this, and then you don't get anything to eat until - if you were invited out to dinner, you were invited for 8 o'clock and you never sat down before 9. I wasn't used to having anything to drink, you know. I'd gone to school during Prohibition. And either I was bored or I was so sleepy that by the time we sat down to dinner - oh. We lived in the French Concession, in an apartment house where we ate in the restaurant, in the dining room, generally.

Q: You girls must have been in much demand. I mean, daughters of the captain.

Mrs. L.: Oh, I wouldn't say that. Nancy was too young. Mary was just a baby. And I don't remember that we did that much partying. I do remember, you know, going out to dinner on the Augusta and going out in the boat and being warned that if you fell into the water and drank one swallow, you'd be dead by the next morning. And we went to Pekin - went to Tsingtao?

Tsingtao, that's right.

Q: That was their base, wasn't it?

Mrs. L.: When did we go up there?

Capt. L.: We spent the summers there.

Mrs. L.: And Nancy and Mother and Mary and I went up on the Shanghai Express. This was just after the Marlene Dietrich movie had come out, and we'd all seen it - or Nancy and I had seen it in the United States. You remember, the band that attacked the train and what not, and it was the first time we'd ever been on a wagon-lits, you know. It was a very palatial arrangements, we thought. Very fancy. We were quite disappointed because no bandits attacked the train. We had to change at a little place called Tsinan Fu, and - who was the girl who had meningitis later on, they had the two children? She was petrified

Capt. L.: (suggests name) Shands (Courtney Shands' wife

Mrs. L.: No, no, no. Oh, she was very pretty. Can't think of her name, but she had two little children and Nancy and I took them in tow ehile we crossed the station - oh, you know. Then, when we got to Pekin, Mother and Dad stayed with the First Secretary of the American Legation - a couple named Spiker. And Nancy and I - I don't know why it was that Mother and Dad stayed with the ~~Ambassador~~ *First Secy.* - but Nancy and I and Admiral and Mrs. Upham were quartered with Nelson Johnson and his wife, who were absolutely the loveliest, most friendly people, and most of the time Nancy and I were going to these official parties. We went, you know, around the city and enjoyed ourselves during the day, and the Minister was absolutely mad about music and he had a wonderful collection of foreign records, and he had his Chinese houseboy - I remember he had Chopin's 24th Preludes, and he had the boy trained to put them on in order. This was the old wind-up Victrola bit. And Nancy and I had many a meal with the boy putting on music for us, you know, while we ate in the big dining room by ourselves. On a couple of occasions, we did have to go out to dinner, we were included and the Admiral had this really obnoxious habit of having the boy - the Admiral and Mrs. Upham and Nancy and I shared a bathroom, and they had these Suchow tubs, you know, and you tell the bath boy and he comes and he pours warm water in the bath. And the Admiral would have the bath boy fill the bath tub, then he'd go down to tea. Well, Nancy and I figured we would skip tea and get our baths and get that out of the way, then we'd be all finished by the time the others came up. So, we got sort of tired of this and held an indignation meeting and we looked out of the window and there they were having tea and having a gorgeous time on the lawn, it was getting later and later and we knew we all had to be ready so we said, we'll take the bath anyway, we'll use the same water.

Q: Stole the Admiral's bath, huh?

Mrs. L.: Yeah. Well, the bath boy had a fit when he saw Nancy and me sneaking down the hall to the bathroom because, "Does de

Admiral's bath." Nancy said, "Yes, we're taking it."

Q: She was a very positive girl, wasn't she?

Mrs. L.: Yeah. She was. But we just - we loved the Johnsons, and when we left instead of writing them a formal bread and butter letter, we wrote them a long piece of doggerel which we later heard they had had framed and hung on their guestroom wall, so we were very honored. We saw them several times in Washington after we all came back there, and he was mentioned in Time magazine rather unkindly - to George Washington University, that is - as the only man who ever graduated from GW and amounted to anything, which is really not fair. They've had some other graduates.

Then we came down from Pekin on the Henderson, remember? You didn't, of course, but we took - um, the only time I ever really got the better of Nancy. We had - we were in our stateroom, we had a light on, and there were still people walking round the deck, I guess, and Nancy was getting undressed and she'd done something that irritated me, or I just decided I'd get my revenge, and I was talking to her and I said, "What did you say, Lieutenant Clark," who was one of the young officers on the Augusta. And Nancy said, "Oh," and dove for the bunk and hit her head on the side and had a lump the size of an egg nexy morning. It was funny, we were sent home - I was going to be 21 on George Washington's birthday of 1935, and so the family, in order not to have to pay my passage back, sent Nancy - oh Nancy was due to go back and start a new term of school, anyway. So they sent us back ahead of time on the

President – Pierce, I guess it was. Anyway, we came back about
– in February and spent the remaining time on the Cape with
my grandmother and my aunt and grandfather until the family
got back. I'd love to go back to China.

Capt. L.: Hong Kong's about the only area you can make it to,
now.

Mrs. L.: Yeah. I wonder what happened to Farmers' Commercial
College for Young Ladies. There was one Belgian girl there –
she and I were determined to speak each other's language. I
wanted to learn idiomatic French and she wanted to learn
English slang, so we would take long walks around Shanghai
and it would be English out and French back, you know. And
when it came to – she had a job all waiting for her, because
both her father and her uncle worked for a French Importing
firm called Olivier Chine, and Andrée was just going to
graduate from this school and go right into a secretarial job.
But she had to have some practice in taking dictation in French,
and of course Mr. Farmer couldn't give it to her. So we had
no French business letters, couldn't find any in the city of
Shanghai, so Andree brought me the Confessions of Jean-Jacques
Rousseau, and I think her French letters – her business
letters – must have been gorgeous. I would sit there, and we
had – the formal opening and closing, she knew, you know, and
how flowery it is, "I beg you to accept the assurance of my
sentiments the most etc." and I would start out, "Dear Monsieur,"
and then a long paragraph from Jean-Jacques Rousseau, while
she criticized my pronunciation and hissed at me between her

teeth, and then we would close with this flowery ending, and I often wonder what kind of letters she wrote for that business - they must have been marvelous.

Q: Did you ever use the training you got?

Mrs. L.: No. The typing, I did. The only trouble is that when you work in a library and you're working on small cards, you lose all your speed, you know. It's just nitpicking, you have to be so careful of spacing.

Q: That was just an illustration of your Mother's...

Mrs. L.: She was just not going to have me sit around and go to pieces in the Orient, the way people did, if you weren't careful. And it is true - you know, she used to worry about this. This was just at the end of the Depression and a lot of these ensigns' wives, this was their first taste of the Navy, and there they were out in the Orient, they didn't even pick up their pajamas, you know, we were getting paid three to one, you know, and Mother used to say, "Oh, they're in for a terrible shock when they get back to the States." And they were. It's funny, Mary who's just so - as Nancy and I used to say, absolutely insufferable when she first came back. She'd walk into a room and say, "My nose is running," you know, in other words, "Amah, where are you?" Yet, she is the one who has ended up, you know, really not a bit interested in any material things, you know, wonderful scientist and, you know, the least likely, it seems to me, of all the family, except she's got this wonderful scientific mind.

Q: She's such a very youthful looking person.

Mrs. L.: Yes. I think a lot of them are, don't you? I mean, I think a nun is ageless.

Q: As I looked at her profile, I thought, of course, it isn't true, but she looked like somebody 20 years old.

Mrs. L.: Uh-huh. I was 17 when she was born and I was a sophomore at the university and I get this casual letter from my Mother saying, "Oh, send me back that dress you said you stepped through the hem of and I will fix it for you. I played nine holes of golf this morning. We had a luncheon for so-and-so," then, "Oh, by the way," and Mother's writing is rather hard to read anyway, and I took this letter to practically every member of the sorority house and I said, "Does that say what I think it does?" And I never saw anyone get more fun out of a baby than Dad did, you know. He was just thrilled to death. I used to be left with Mary when she was pretty brand new and I'd never picked up a baby in my life before. Mother'd be at some luncheon in San Diego and Dad would be at his office ashore, and Mary would start to yell, and I'd panic, and I'd call up the office and say, "The baby's crying. What'll I do?" And Dad would say, "Pat her on the back. Don't be silly. Pick her up and pat her on the back."

Q: Did you say earlier that you were out in California at the time of his death?

Mrs. L.: Yes.

Q: Did you see him...?

Mrs. L.: No, no. This is another - I know that we all sort of understood that this was imminent. We didn't know how imminent and I had this week and it seemed like a good time, you know, for us to go out, and by the time Dick and I got there, Dad was really not conscious and that first evening Mother said to me very honestly, "Now, I want to say this to you. If you really insist on seeing your Father, that's all right. But I really think you would be happier if you didn't." And I must tell you that I was very relieved that she said this, because the last time I saw my Father, he and Mother had just visited us, and they were leaving, and he was standing on our bottom step, and he said, "Marvelous time. Godbye. See you next year," or something, and that's the way I remember him. I did not see him. See, we got out there...

Capt. L.: On Saturday.

Mrs. L.: On Saturday - and when did he die?

Capt. L.: On Sunday.

Mrs. L.: Yeah. There were a lot of things about Irish Catholic Newport that I will never understand, but one of the things is the, I think, terrible custom of wakes. At school, a teacher will say, "Oh, I have to go to three wakes," or, and they always have an open casket and all this business. So the first thing they all wanted to know when I got back to school, and I thought this was (a) an impertinent question, but they didn't regard it as such, I mean they didn't mean it this way, but they just hoped I got there in time, and I knew that this meant to them, you know, was I there when he died and, you know, how about a few details. I just will never understand this.

Q: Well, it's not a part of your culture, and it wasn't part of his culture.

Mrs. L.: No. It is. It is. I know, the open casket and -- We had a student at school who -- a little boy who hanged himself. Obviously, he was a very much disturbed kid and his homeroom teacher told us that she had gone to the wake and that he looked so strange, you know, and I said, "Don't tell me that after this kind of a thing they would have an open casket." And she said coldly, "That's the way we do things," and so I stopped, it's just not my business.

The afternoon that Dad died I took Gigi to walk. Gigi was just so enchanted to see me. Nancy or Augie or I could always take Gigi around the base, you know, and we went down - do you know Treasure Island, you know as you walk down, there are all these deserted buildings from World War I, it's really creepy, decayed atmosphere down there, and it was foggy, and Gigi who had never done anything like this before, I was doing the regular walk that she and I - and Dad and she always did, right around the point, when all of a sudden that miserable dog was on the outboard side and she saw something that intrigued her and she plunged down into the current, and it's very fast at that point, and it was cold as ice, and I thought, "Oh," you know, "if I come back without that dog," I peeled off my shoes and nylons and started down over these sharp rocks, yelling at Gigi who, I could see, was having a little trouble at this point swimming against the current. I was panicky and there wasn't anybody around there. Finally, when I was just about to go in myself - that would have been smart, I, you know, it was probably over my head - she turned and made for the shore. So we got up to the house and the Filipino boys were out there, you know, looking very horrified, and Mother had just gotten into an afternoon dress and just shortly after we got back, Dr. Corbin came in and said he thought that Dad was - had taken a turn for the worse and they called the doctor, and it was very shortly after that that he died. He never did regain consciousness.

The funeral had, I hate to say it, was rather grotesque actually. It was a beautiful service, but I mean there were always these - the Filipino boys seemed to have a sixth sense as to when it was a crank call and they'd call me instead of Mother. Nancy had just gone back. She had been up there during most of the week, and she'd just gone back to Topanga, and he died that night, and we called her and she came right back the next day. But, of course, the telephone calls began to pour in, and some of them were really very strange, they really were. A weird woman in San Francisco who asked for Mother and, as I say, the boys just seemed to have this sixth sense, you know, and they'd call me - and I don't know whether she was just a mentally off or loaded or what, but very morbid, and finally I just hung up on her, you know.

Q: Well, that whole service, all the arrangements he had made himself, hadn't he?

Mrs. L.: It was a very, very simple, and it was really lovely, and the long trip down to the cemetery, you know, every time we went under an overpass, it was just ringed, lined with people, mostly ex-service or service men who had been waiting for hours for us, and one of the things I remember, as we came into the cemetery, Mother had, you know, men from all the services standing at attention, I remember, a sailor who couldn't have been old enough to have served with Daddy, he didn't look as old as Dick, who was   , standing there with, you know, he was so stiff that his back was arched and he had tears just streaming down his cheeks, and I know he never could have served with Daddy. He was much too young. But one of the grotesque things that happened was that there was a very portly Marine, you know, they had all the services represented and they were standing holding the flag, and this Marine who apparently hadn't been in his uniform for some time and he was standing rigidly at attention, and all of a sudden his belt just went pop and dropped onto the ground, and the man who was in charge of the cemetery was horrified and snatched it up. Just the touch that shouldn't have happened.

Q: Poor man, he breathed.

Mrs. L.: Yeah. Poor man, he breathed. I think Admiral Spruance is buried right next to Dad, isn't he?

Q: Was that not your Father's plan?

Mrs. L.: I think they all sort of...

Q: Lockwood and Spruance and himself...

Mrs. L.: The conferences that are going to go on.

Q: Tell me about the Admiral coming back to dedicate the Raytheon plant.

Capt. L.: Well, this was in October 1960, if I remember rightly, and he was invited to make the principal address. He made a very good address and, of course, the Governor was here, and Charles Francis Adams, and, oh, a whole raft of dignitaries, and we had a big reception afterwards. We had a great big circus tent out in front and we had a dinner in a cafeteria which I wouldn't say was...

Mrs. L.: Lunkheon.

Capt. L.: Luncheon, that's right.....wasn't fabulous. All the Raytheon vice presidents and Charles Francis Adams were all there, and the Admiral sat Next to Mr. Hamel. Mr. Hamel was General Manager of the plant when we opened down here. What else can be added to that?

Mrs. L.: I really can't add anything. We were, of course, delighted when they asked him because it meant that we got to see them.

Q: And you say that the plant has to do with submarines.

Capt. L.: We make the sonar for the nuclear attack submarines.

Q: I see, and of course this is an area where the Admiral was most interested.

Capt. L.: He was a submariner earlier, you see. And then we have a big plaque out there in the lobby to the effect that he dedicated it.

Mrs. L.: Remember when we went over to Quonset to meet him, the plane came in there and...

Capt. L.: Charles Francis Adams in the plane

Mrs. L.: coming over on the ferry, he remarked that as a very junior officer he had been up here, I think, taking diving lessons, you know, and they used to get an old chief who used to send them down to the bottom of the Sakonnet River and make them stay down there until they'd speared x number of flounder, and when you had x number of flounder you could come up, and the chief confiscated the fish. [I remember bawling the heck out of him.] Is he still living?

Capt. L.: I think so.

Mrs. L.: Well, while we have it here. I think the second time, the first time he was here at the house he had word that the Edies were celebrating their anniversary. This was a Congressional Medal of Honor, I think...

Capt. L.: Yes.

Mrs. L.: ...and he was one of the people that dived for the S-51, wasn't he? or - what was the...?

Q: Out in the Pacific?

Mrs. L.: Oh, no. The S-51 was the one that was rammed by the City of Rome at Narraganset here, what, in about 1929?

Anyway, Edie had a Congressional Medal of Honor, and he's now a very elderly man, he lives here in Newport, and Dad sent him a congratulatory telegram, and we see Edie occasionally at the Navy League. But he was one of the Navy's earliest divers. Dad remembered him quite well.

Capt. L.: And knew him by sight when he saw him.

Mrs. L.: Yes, he did. That was another thing about Daddy, he very rarely forgot people and faces.

Q: How did he achieve that?

Mrs. L.: I don't know. I don't know. He was terrible with remembering how many times people had been married. Mother used to say to him, "For Heaven's sake,, darling, when you see so-and-so at the party to night, don't say to his wife, it's a long time since old so-and-so days because this is not the same wife." Daddy couldn't remember. I've done this myself. It makes one feel awful.

Q: Is there a copy of his speech here? At this dedication?

Capt. L.: I imagine they have one on file. I don't think we have one here.

Mrs. L.: I don't think we do, either. I wouldn't think it would contribute much to the

Q: It wouldn't?

Mrs. L.: I don't think so. I mean, it would be one of these official -- I don't think it would be anything that, you know, would throw any new light.

Q: Have you, during the course of the evening, thought of any of those stories?

Mrs. L.: No.

Q: Unprintable ones?

Mrs. L.: I don't think he had any unprintable, really.

Capt. L.: They were always just on the edge.

Mrs. L.: Right on the edge. Yeah. Uh-huh.

Capt. L.: Carefully selected.

Mrs. L.: Sorry, I just am drawing a blank, and it's not because I'm afraid to repeat them. I just can't think of any. Nancy and Mother must have given you plenty, though. Or Chet.

Q: No, he didn't tell me any. At that stage, I wasn't thinking in terms of...

Mrs. L.: When did you talk to Chet?

Q: Oh, last April, up in New Canaan.

Mrs. L.: Oh, at their house?

Q: Yes.

Mrs. L.: Isn't that a lovely house? Did you meet any of the

girls?

Q: No.

Mrs. L.: I think they're all in school.

Q: He and his wife were there alone. Well, I will ask you something that I asked Nancy, and she answered it, too. Your Mother objected.

Mrs. L.: About my ~~aunts~~. Father?

Q: I said, that, of course, your Father was noted for his even temper, for his high standards, and almost for his perfection in everything he did. But a biographer is going to have an awfully tough time writing a life of a man who was perfection and nothing less...

Mrs. L.: Oh, ridiculous.

Q: ...and so I asked Nancy if she could think of any weaknesses in his makeup.

Mrs. L.: And what was her reply?

Q: And she did think of something, and your Mother objected to it...

Mrs. L.: What was it? I'm just curious.

Q: Nancy talked about, in retirement, how impatient and irritable he sometimes got...

Mrs. L.: He did. That's very true.

Q: ...and went on to elucidate on that.

Mrs. L.: Yes, that was very true. This person who had been so tranquil and serene - I guess, felt that he had to part somewhere because he did, and he got very depressed at times, which he had never done before. One of the things that I couldn't understand was, Jay was ordered to the <u>Helena</u>. We went out in November of '57 and they insisted that we stay with them. The <u>Helena</u> was being overhauled at Long [Mare?] Island, and, you know, I thought this would be lovely for Thanksgiving, but that we should/then get an apartment in Berkeley because I knew what it would be like with three kids, you know. By this time, my Mother had really gotten things down to a fine art. That house was run for Dad and nothing was allowed, you see, and something had to give, you know. You have three kids in there. I just figured they couldn't live up to this and...

Q: It would break the routine.

Mrs. L.: That's right, and this was absolutely right. And the first thing was that it seemed to me that he just seemed to get more glum, more depressed as Christmas approached, and Mother said to me, "You know what it is. He's lost 50 per cent, you know, of his very dearest friends at Pearl Harbor. He's been like this at Christmas ever since." And I said, "Oh, come on." She said, "No, it's true." He was never irritable with the kids, but he just - this is - he was in many respects a different person. Always very, very sweet to all of us, but you could see that, for instance, Mother was the one who really got worried about him. I think she worried unduly, to the point where she let him get away with what - she was the one who said, "I'm glad he's got a dog, because a dog is a one - Dinah was-with quite a personality of her own. A dog is one thing that isn't afraid of a Fleet Admiral and that, you know, is not going to cater to his whims, and she's going to lead him a merry chase and it's good for him." But the kids would come home from school and they'd have some of their friends with them and, you know, I'd soft pedalled this for the first couple of weeks we were there, and saying all the time, "We've got to get an apartment," and "Oh, no, no. Your Father would be terribly hurt," and so forth. But I could see that it bothered her. They'd bring all their friends and they wanted to come in and watch television, or they wandered all around the garden, and this was a house that was just no longer geared to kids. Things like Admiral Toyoda's sword, which was as sharp as a razor, lying ready for anybody to pick it up, you know. And maybe disturbing the routine and...

Capt. L.: The routine having to run on schedule, too.

Mrs. L.: Oh, yes. He got absolutely neurotic about time. Nancy must have told you that. I'm sort of neurotic about time, too. I mean, if somebody says I'm going to meet you at 9 o'clock, damit, you'd better be there, because I was brought up this way, but Dad got to the point where if he said, "We will leave at 9," he was irritated if you weren't ready to leave at quarter of. I mean, he was tapping his foot, and this was very hard to live with, you know, and also I felt sorry for Mother because there'd be a group of people there, and Dad would all of a sudden decide that he had it - he'd get up and leave, you know, and just very quietly go out and go to bed.

Q: She had to deal with them!

Mrs. L.: Yeah. Well, even at the Observatory, Nancy and I used to kid him about this. He had a movie of the Eruption of Krakatoa and whenever he got really fed up with a dinner party or something, he'd tell the boys to come and bring that wonderful movie of and then he'd sit in the back and go to sleep or he'd sneak out. He did sort of the same thing with records, much earlier, when we lived in Chevy Chase, there was a captain whose wife never stopped yaking, and they lived right in the neighborhood, and she'd drop in, and she'd start. Dad would say, "Oh, are you fond of music?" "Oh, yes, I love music." Well, the girls have a beautiful new recording of the Beethoven Violin Concerto and, "Catherine or Nancy, get that beautiful voilin concerto and put it on," and then he could sort of imply that everybody'd better be quiet, and she would stand it as long as she could and then they would get up and leave.

Q: That didn't last for 50 minutes!

Mrs. L.: But he did, he got very, very antsy, that's true, and this was - I think Mother was, Mother is without a doubt the most successful wife that I have ever met in my life, because without being a Christian martyr about it, she really did, you know, keep everything on an even keel, she really did.

wouldn't listen to what anybody had to say, and Mother would have to raise her voice so that he didn't, you know repeat all the conversation after the party was over, and she'd say, "Why don't you listen?" "Well, people mutter." But this is true. But I never saw him impatient with the kids - never.

Q: Well, as I said earlier, I think she's a remarkable person.

Mrs. L.: She is.

Q: I think she's a great woman.

Mrs. L.: Their backgrounds were absolutely different, completely different, and I think temperamentally they were very different, but they certainly were happy.

Q: And she succeeded in keeping pace with him on all these different levels, which is so utterly remarkable.

Mrs. L. Yeah.

Capt. L: Could adapt herself to any situation.

Mrs. L.: Mother didn't want that   that's right. I sort of half expected that she would say to me, "Now, remember, you must be discreet." But she didn't. I said,, "What kind of material is Mr. Mason / interested in?" and she said, "Anything to do with your Father," and she didn't add any caution or look-out or...

Q: I think she's enthusiastic about this biography.

Mrs. L.: But, you know, this business of how he'd never have it written during his lifetime, he would never record any of his own reminiscences, and she asked me yesterday, "Has Mr. Potter been approached or had officers say to him, 'Oh, you're not going to say anything mean about anybody, are you?'" I wondered if he had, you know, because...

Q: He hasn't to my knowledge...

Mrs. L.: I said, "Gee, Mother, you know, you're talking to a librarian now. I mean, a person who's doing a biography has to be objective." Dad was a very unmalicious person himself. I made another absolutely fantastic boner, quite innocently. A class party up at Providence, I forget whose party it was, somebody came up to me -- people are always doing this -- and said to me, "What did your father really think about, you know, so-and-so," and usually I'm smart enough to say, "Well, I never really heard him say." And in most cases I never did. So this person came up to me and said, after I'd had two drinks, and said, "Hey, you know, I've always really wondered, what did your father really think of so-and so?" And I said, "I never really heard him say," then I spoiled the effect completely by saying reflectively, "You know, my Father always said, if you can't say anything nice about somebody, don't say anything." That was really   ho-hum. But you know I do not remember ever hearing him, when we were sitting around the table in the bosom of the family, criticize...

Capt. L.: Never.

Mrs. L.: I just don't. He would talk about office matters at home and Mother would look around severely at Nancy and me, "You are not to discuss this outside the house," and Nancy and I, who couldn't have been less interested at this point, we were both working in the library, and we'd say, "Oh, tell us some more, so we can go and talk about it." After I got married to Jay and we were, you know, his senior officers – a lot of them – were the people that I knew had worked with Dad, I could have kicked myself for not remembering some of these things that Dad had said. I'd say, "Well, I know Dad worked with him in such-and-such a job, but I can't remember," and then I was rather sorry I hadn't paid more attention. But Mother was always afraid that we would go out and say something indiscreet, you know. But we weren't that interested.

Q: I've seen many of his letters written in retirement, and he did comment, not in a derogatory way, but he commented quite frankly on world events.

Mrs. L.: Oh, yes, he did.

Q: And was quite opinionated about this subject or that subject.

Mrs. L.: He always made it a point to say that he was not expressing the sentiments of the U.S. Navy, which some retired people haven't been astute enough to do. I mean, he always made it a point that this was his own opinion and not anybody's else's.

Q: One thing that Ned is most interested in finding out is

the Admiral's reaction to - at the time of some of the crucial battles in the Pacific - how did he react.

Mrs. L.: Yes, well, Mother would have had that. Mother would be the one...

Capt. L.: She was on the Coast when...

Mrs. L.: Yes, but I mean he was writing Mother every day, and he was using her as a safety valve. She might...

Q: Well, Ned's going to see her in March or April, or some time, so maybe he'll ask some of those questions.

Mrs. L.: Yeah. I would think that that would be the thing. I - I mean at the time he never would have written to Nancy and me, because it was too near the event. He commented - wrote to us afterwards - I think this is one of the stories he told the boys - the business about the misunderstanding about where his Task Force 38, the world wants to know - you remember that. That was padding and Halsey considered it insulting. It was never meant that way. He told us the story. I think he did square it later on. The misunderstanding was cleared up. That was something that we never knew until after the war.

Capt. L.: They used a padding for every message at the beginning and the end. It was supposed to be something not even associated with the message, and they just made a poor choice of words when they padded that one.

Q: Because it just tied on to the...

Capt. L.: It was similar to the theme and the fellow decoding it just left it on.

Mrs. L.: I never met Admiral Halsey. I would love to have. We have a biography of him for young - for junior high school age group - in the library and it's very popular I would say with the Navy juniors, mainly, you know. He was a colorful figure to their fathers. These kids don't remember him, of course, but they've heard enough about him from their fathers, so that they want to read about him.

Q: I would judge that from all the - from all I've heard and read, that your Father's real favorite was Spruance.

Mrs. L.: Oh, no question about it.

Q: They were really compatible.

Mrs. L.: No question about it.

Q: He told me he felt he could depend on him, too.

Mrs. L.: Was Nat [Ned (Spruance)] a classmate of Chet's? Yes, wasn't he? '36? Admiral Spruance's son, the one who was killed recently?

Capt. L.: Yes, I think so.

Mrs. L.: I met him and his wife briefly the first time I went to Treasure Island. They were still stationed on the island.

Q: Do you have a story now? One of your Father's stories.

Mrs. L.: This story concerns a town which was overrun with cats.

They had a terrible time, and so with great desperation, they decided to hire a consultant, and they found this man who, like the Pied Piper, said he would rid the town of cats, but it would be very expensive and he named some colossal fee. They agreed to this. They were so desperate. So he spent a few days in town, and finally came back with his report, and said, "You see that great big tom cat up there." And they said, "Oh, yes. That's an old tom. He's sort of a town mascot." "That's your trouble. Get rid of him." And they said, "Oh, we wouldn't do that. We'll have him altered." So they did, and the population of cats decreased and they paid the consultant this huge sum of money. And in a very short time, the problem manifested itself again, and the cats began reappearing, and they were outraged and they sent for the consultant and said he was a fraud. He said, "No. I gave you the right answer. You just didn't handle it right." They said, "You told us that old tom was ourpproblem, and to get rid of him, and we had him altered." He said, "Yes, but now he's acting as consultant."

Q: Thank you for that story.

Mrs. L.: I think it's pretty generally known.

INDEX

for an interview

with

CAPTAIN AND MRS. JAMES T. LAY

Adams, Charles Francis, 110-111

Adventure, 71

Air Force, 67

Aquinas, Sister Mary (Nimitz) 20, 26, 36-37, 39-41, 45, 64, 76, 98-100, 104-105

Arizona, 46

Augusta, 1-3, 5, 7-14, 54, 79, 86, 95, 97-99, 102

Benevolence, 73

Berkeley, 30-32, 43, 92-93

Buck, 20

California, 30

California, University of, 9, 31-32, 41, 91

Canaga, Captain Bruce, 89

Carnegie, Dale, 61-62

Carter, G. O., 89

China, 1-3, 40, 54, 98, 103

Conolly, Admiral Richard L., 17-18

Corbin, Dr., 108

Court, Captain Alvah Breaker, 87

Duke of York, 74

Eadie, Thomas, 111-112

Eisenhower, President and Mrs. Dwight D., 78

Forrestal, James, 80

Fraser, Admiral Sir Bruce, 74

Funeral, 108-109

Furlong, Admiral William Rea, 88-89

General Sturgis, 21

Gigi, 107-108

Griller, Sidney, 44

Guam, 19

Gygax, Admiral Felix Xerxes, 13-14

Halsey, Admiral William Frederick, 21, 82-83, 121-122

Harvard, 41

Helena, 115

Henderson, 102

Honolulu, 25-26, 47

Iwo Jima campaign, 64

Jackson, Admiral Richard Harrison, 39

Japan, 6-8

Japanese, 54; surrender, 73-75

Johnson, Nelson and Mrs., 100, 102

Joy, Admiral C. Turner, 16-17

Jutland, Battle of, 27-28

Kobe, 7, 9-10

Lamar, Capt. Howell A., 79

Leverton, Bill and Helen, 96-97

Life, 65

Lockwood, Admiral Charles Andrews, 110

Louisville, 16-18

MacArthur, General and Mrs. Douglas, 72-73

Manila Bay, 5

Melbourne, 12

Midway, Battle of, 67

Mikasa, 25

Morgan, Gwen, 61, 63

Music, 42-45

Naval Academy, 40, 68, 71, 86-88

Naval Institute, 33

Naval War College, 27-29

Newport, 26-28

Nimitz, Mrs. Chester W., 25-26, 28-29, 33, 38, 41-42, 45, 47, 49-50, 52, 54, 57, 62-63, 69-71, 74-79, 81-82, 86-91, 98, 100, 104-105, 108, 113-121

Nimitz, Chester W., Jr., 25, 28-30, 40, 43-45, 50, 57, 70-71, 79, 92, 113, 122

Nimitz, Grandmother, 34

Nimitz, Joan, 47

Nimitz, Aunt Louisa, 35

Nimitz, Mary (see Aquinas)

Nimitz, Nancy, 16, 26, 32, 34, 36, 41, 43, 46-49, 54, 56, 60-63, 69, 74-74, 78-79, 93, 98-102, 107-108, 113-114, 117, 120-121

Nimitz, Otto, 27, 34-35

NROTC, 30, 32

Oahu, 18

Observatory House, 22-23, 55, 76, 117

Ohio, 24

Okinawa, 19

Orleck, 81

Patrick, RADM Goldsborough S., 14

Pearce, Edward S., 7

Pearl Harbor, 16, 18, 47, 56-57

Pearson, Drew, 66

Portland, 1-2

Potter, Professor E. B., 119-120

President Johnson, 98

President Pierce, 103

Proceedings, 33

Puleston, Captain William D., 52-53

Reading, 25-26

Rigel, 36-37, 40, 68

Robison, Admiral S. S., 30

Ruark, Robert, 67

San Pedro, 29-30

Schenck, 15

Senn, Admiral and Mrs. Thomas Jones, 38

Shanghai, 10-11, 98-100, 103

Spruance, Admiral Raymond Ames, 18, 60, 109-110, 122

Stories, 78-79, 122-123

Swimming, 18

Sydney, 12

Togo, Admiral Heihachiro, 8-9, 24-25

Tokyo Bay, 20, 73

Treasure Island, 33, 107, 122

Trenton, 46

Truman, President Harry, 67

Tsingtao, 9-11, 99-100

Turner, Admiral Kelly, 19

United Nations, 89-90

Upham, Admiral and Mrs. F. B., 9, 100-102

Waters, Admiral and Mrs. Odale, 96-97

Wilkinson, Admiral Theodore Stark, 18-19, 21

World War II, 16-20, 56-60, 64, 67-68; Japanese surrender, 73-74

Yale, 41

Yokohama, 9, 73

Interview with Sister Aquinas, daughter of Fleet Admiral Nimitz at her mother's apartment in San Francisco

Date: 4 June 1969

By: John T. Mason, Jr.

Subject: Admiral Chester Nimitz

Q: Sister Aquinas, I'm so delighted that you've consented to give me your recollections of your father. Would you begin by talking about your very early childhood, as the daughter of a Navy family, and as the youngest child in the family. This obviously brought you certain advantages.

Sister A.: Well, it brought me advantages in that I had my brother and sisters to help raise me. I understand, although I was too young to remember, that they volunteered once that I should be the smartest of them all because I had their help.

Q: You mean you had the benefit of their...

Sister A.: I had the benefit of their experience.

Q: That was very generous of them, wasn't it? And has it turned out that way?

Sister A.: I don't think so.

Q: You have a long time before you to prove this.

Sister A.: That's true, but I suspect that...

Mrs. N. You're the only doctor in the family.

Sister A.: Yes, I may have the only doctorate in the family.

But that's not saying that the others couldn't get them three times over.

My earliest recollections of being a member of a naval family come from China, where I just vaguely remember playing on a bamboo jungle jim and leaping off. I remember seeing the thing shake behind me. I was a substantial child.

Q: Did you see much of your father at that time?

Sister A.: I don't really recall that much. I have no recollections of...

Mrs. N.: You were very annoyed at finding you had to live in a house after having lived on a ship. She thought she was going to live on the *Augusta*, you see.

Sister A.: After my early first two years on the ship, and pulling kittens' tails like fury, judging from the pictures I have, which they say are me. One of the consequences of having lived in China was when I came back at the age of four and went to nursery school across the street in Washington D.C., when we lived on Kirk Street, wasn't it?

Mrs. N.: Yes.

Sister A.: I came home, I am told, simply refusing to go back to nursery school again, and through enquiries it seems that the other children were making fun of my pidgin English.

Mrs. N.: She put Chinese construction on everything, and she was so hurt when they made fun of her that she would not go back to the school.

Sister A.: The other consequence, my mother tells me, was my fascination later for wearing pink and red together, in the days before such things were acceptable.

Q: Quite acceptable now. It's um fortunate that you can't wear them now.

Sister A.: The next, better memories would be when Daddy was stationed, wasn't he station on the Trenton, no that was on the Arizona when Mary...

Mrs. N.: Yes, on the Arizona.

Sister A.: And I do remember he would come walking on the beach with me a lot, and we used to go down about a mile and rent, it was just a sort of a half surfboard, just a narrow board, and then ride the waves. It was great sport.

Q: He was a great walker, wasn't he, on the beach?

Sister A.: Oh, very much so. He walked all the time. The other place where I remember him walking a great deal was in Berkeley. This would be after he bought a house there. We'd walk up to the Berkeley dog-run - up in the Tilden Park area - actually, it's been named the Nimitz Way for him since. He used to scatter yellow lupin seeds...

Q: Lupin seeds?

Sister A.: Lupin, ah huh.

Sister A. - 4

Q: Was he fond of lupins?

Sister A.: He was fond of all wild flowers.

Mrs. N.: You may not have ever seen the yellow lupin. It grows in big shrubs.

Q: Is this a Texas...?

Mrs. N.: No, no, it's a California flower, but only in the fog areas. It won't grow anywhere else.

Q: Well, he took you along on these walks. Was this designed for companionship.

Sister A.: Yes, just for fun.

Mrs. N.: Not only Mary, but all of the girls that stayed with us.

Q: He was fond of children?

Sister A.: Oh, yes. Very much so. Another memory from that era touches on one of our neighbors who lived on 1618 East Ocean Avenue with us. The Admiral Shaffroth, and he was always very fond of all of the Nimitz children, and at various times - well, at one point, gave me four turtles, which I - perhaps a dubious honor to his family - named after the members of it. Then one Christmas, Admiral Shaffroth told me that Santa Claus had left something down in his apartment for me, and if I would come by later and get it, I could have it. And my innocent remark in reply was, "I wonder how Santa Claus ever could have made such a mistake, as leaving it at the wrong

Sister A. - 5

apartment."

Q: That's gratitude for you, wasn't it?

Sister A.: It must have been shortly after that when we went back to Washington D.C. and Daddy was Chief of the Bureau of Navigation. No, the shells came after he went back to the Pacific, that's right, and Admiral Calhoun, who was then, I think stationed on Guam, sent me...

Mrs. N.: No, he was stationed in Honolulu.

Sister A.: That's right, yes. He sent me a group of shells which very much intrigued me and within the week Mother had gotten me a book for children on sea shells. I was about seven at the time, no, about ten, and the book suggested that one of the shells that I had quite a few specimens of was quite rare. So Mother took me to the National Museum and we checked this out and found it wasn't at all rare, but anyhow it started me off on a hobby which Daddy and Mother fostered all along. Many of Daddy's friends in the Pacific sent me shells, and several times during the war, I let it be known that there was either a book or a sea shell that he wanted and, sure enough, it turned up.

Q: You certainly had plenty of contacts.

Sister A.: Yes.

Q: People who were traveling all over were apt to bring something.

Sister A. - 6

Sister A.: There was one book he was trying to get, it was a Japanese book, on shells by a man whose name Daddy thought was Hirose ~~Herapi~~. The first book they sent him was not Hirose's but concerned [f?] It was sort of a temporary measure, out of a library and came shell that had been bombed out in Palau, wasn't it?

Mrs. N.: Palau.

Sister A.: They sent me a book on shells and fish, marine life in general, with the explanation that they were also still looking for the other book. Well, finally, when they found it, they discovered the man's name was Hirose, and not ~~Herapi~~ Hirose, and that was supposed to make a great deal of difference in Japanese. It was like confusing Smith and Brown here, perhaps.

Q: Do you know why your Father and Mother fostered this interest of yours?

Mrs. N.: We fosterdd whatever the children were interested in.

Sister A.: Yes. Whatever interest we manifested, they took it up and saw to it that...

Q: This was a part of their attitude toward your growing up?

SisterA.: Very much.

Q: Anything that you showed an aptitude for, that they...

Sister A.: Right. Even after the time came when I no longer had much time to work with my sea shells, Daddy continued to be interested and - well, within the last two or three years before he died, he obtained three Golden Cowries for me.

Sister A. - 7

He had heard from someone that the Golden Cowry that had been brought to me originally was a very beach-worn specimen, and he put out a search notice and, within a very short time, he had three specimens, one of which has since been given to the California Academy of Sciences, but two of which I still have in my collection, and they were obtained, one at Ponape, and one at Guam. The original Cowry came from Guam and had been brought to me by a Commodore Grant. Commodore Grant arranged to bring them one day when Daddy was home for conferences during World War II - it must have been 1944 or 1945, because that was the year I was in the eighth grade at the convent - and a very humorous story is connected with that. We had told the Sister who was answering the door that Commodore Grant was expected, and this Sister - Sister Bede - when Commodore Grant (?) came, indeed let him in and indicated that he was out in the summer house...

Q: That your father was out...

Sister A.: Yes, that my father was out in the summer house visiting with me, and so Commodore Grant came with -

Mrs. N.: Grant.

Sister A.: Grant, that's right - came with this little basket, very attractive straw basket of shells, and as soon as Sister Bede had left Commodore Grant and had gone back about her business, one of the older Sisters - Sister Bernadine - who was very much a figure in the community, grabbed her and said, "How do you know that that man isn't a spy come to do the

Sister A. - 8

Admiral harm?" So, I guess Sister Bede assured her that we had expected him.

Q: Sister, let me ask you at this point, in terms of your education and in terms of the vocation you found, how you happened to go to a convent school?

Sister A.: Well, I think - it's my understanding that the reason was that it was fairly certain that after the war I would be going back - we'd probably be going back to the East Coast for duty, and since schools in the East, at that time, anyhow, tended to be roughly half a year to a year ahead of what they [west coast schools] were teaching. I think Mother's interest was to make sure that I would be taught so I could keep up.

Mrs. N.: It was also because when I sent her to the Anna Head School, which at that time was headed by a very weak pair, I arranged for them, because I had to be at the hospital all day, for Mary, who was a day student, to be taken care of in the afternoon until 5 o'clock. I paid extra for it. Time after time, I came home and found Mary had been home all the afternoon alone, and when I'd say, "Why did they send you home?" she'd say, "Well, because the lady that was supposed to take care of us wanted to go to San Francisco for the afternoon." Well, there was a danger, and the Navy felt it, of Mary being kidnapped by somebody who wanted to upset the Admiral, you see, because she was young. So I decided that the only way she'd be safe was to put her in the convent. I'd known of this school for years, and I assure you nobody could have gotten anywhere near Mary. They took wonderful care of

Sister A. - 9

her, and it has a very high scholastic rating.

Sister A.: Perhaps we might pursue right there - you asked about Daddy's attitude toward our education. They both definitely had a belief in doing the best by us they can, and then letting us make our own decisions. So, when I finally indicated to them that I did want to go into the convent, they were certainly the most gracious of parents. Far more gracious than many of my Catholic parents - my friends' Catholic parents - ever were. Far more understanding. And there was, after the news reached the papers - and I even forget how that came about...

Mrs. N.: It came about because we were at a dinner party and some friends who happened to be there asked me and I happened to remark and somebody heard it and told the papers that she was going in the convent.- going in the next day. And that was very unpleasant.

Q: When did you make that decision?

Sister A.: Well, I thought about it during most of Stanford. I really had the idea from the time I was a junior in high school, toward the end of the junior year. And Mother and Daddy asked me to wait before becoming a Catholic for a year, to be sure that that was what I really wanted. Then I did graduate from Stanford and I actually started on a master's program there, but after about three weeks - I told you at Christmas time - that I wanted to go in the following July, and it became obvious to me that it would be both nice from the point of view that I could live with them the last six months, if I transferred to the University of California, and also...

Mrs. N.: You'd finished your course.

Sister A.: Yes, I'd finished my course in June. And it was also much more likely that I would be sent back to finish my education if I had been at Cal, because of the fact that it was a state school and the tuition was less. That was a very enjoyable six months, too, as I recall. One of the more choice memories of that six months - I don't know how Daddy felt about it, but I sure know how Mother did - was when they were going out one evening and I had borrowed my neighbor's microscope and was working on an experiment for this invertebrate physiology course I was taking, and as Mother went by the door, she saw me scuttle something out of her sight, and she asked me what it was I was working with. I had to confess it was cockroaches, and I was told that if there were any cockroaches loose in the house when she came back, I could expect to leave.

Q: Pack your bag and go, before the six months were up.

Mrs. N.: I had 36 custard cups...

Sister A.: And I raised my salamanders in them the same semester. I was taking a course on the natural history of vertebrates, and I took as my project of watching the early development of salamander larvae, so I appropriated my mother's 36 custard

Sister A. - 11

cups to raise the salamanders in, which also shows how remarkably tolerant she was. All this sort of thing.

Q: Your father was really interested in the scientific end of your...?

Sister A.: Oh, yes.

Mrs. N.: Tell him about your meeting the Battha girl your last year in the convent.

Sister A.: Yes, the last year I was at the convent - well, actually, it was just toward the end of my junior year in high school when the convent authorities brought around one day for all of us students to meet, 4 Hungarian girls who had just come over from - oh, I guess they had just come from Switzerland, actually - they had left Hungary just ahead of the Germans, wasn't it?

Mrs. N. No, it was just ahead of the Russians.

Sister A.: Was it the Russians? This would have been back in 1948, 1947 or 1948. So it was earlier than during the revolt. And we were told that these four girls would be coming to school with us the following year. One of them was in my class. The names of the four were Maria, Magda, Margit, and Marta, and Magda was in my class. They were in this country under the auspices of the Pope's Children's War Relief, wasn't it? Isn't that what it was called?

Mrs. N. Yes.

Sister A - 12

Sister A.: Anyway, it was the Pope's Children something or other. But their guardians turned out to be rather severe women, and the Batthas were none too keen, and it became progressively more true that they became none too keen on going home to them during vacations, and so they began coming home with me and, in essence, at that point, Mother and Daddy acquired four more children.

Mrs. N.: They came for Christmas, Thanksgiving. They all had keys to the house. At weekends we never knew how many children we were going to have in, because they'd all come from all over.

Sister A.: In the end, Daddy was also very much instrumental in expediting their becoming citizens. Because, didn't he actually arrange for the passage of a special bill through Congress to make sure that they would get in?

Mrs. N.: Yes.

Q: Without having to wait for the quota?

Sister A.: Yes, I think that was the problem. The quota had been filled for that year.

Mrs. N.: Well, he marched three of them up the aisle.

Sister A.: Three of them? That's right Marta, Margit, and Magda.

Mrs. N. He marched them up the aisle. We now have what I call my seven foster grandchildren.

Sister A. - 13

Q: You mean he gave them away?

Mrs. N.: Yes.

Sister A.: Oh, one of the things Daddy and Mother did at that time when news of my ~~trying for~~ entering the community first got out, was to prevent a great deal of the unpleasant telephone calls, correspondents, and so forth, from ever reaching me. I didn't know about this for a long time afterwards. But they did.

Q: From prejudiced people and things like that.

Mrs. N.: Do you know that people came up to our house at night and stuffed things under the door, doing all sorts of things, and we never gave them to Mary. We just kept them away from her, and the day she went into the convent, Mother Margaret had called me in the morning and said, "Oh, they're over here waiting for Mary, and I've told them she isn't coming in till after noon. Now they've just started over for your house." And I said,, "Fine we'll start over for the convent." So we passed all these newspaper people going this way and we were going the other way, and they didn't recognize her. I was driving.

Q: Had you anticipated some of that?

Mrs. N.: Yes. We thought this might come up, and we got her in there safely. While she was in the novitiate she used to drive the bus to pick up the children...

Sister A.: But they wouldn't let me do it for the first three

Sister A. - 14

months.

Mrs. N.: No, but when they did, they finally had to take her off because...

Sister A.: No, I did it the full time.

Mrs. N.: Yes, but didn't you - you had one time when you found that they were going to chase it, going to catch hold of it...

Sister A.: No.

Mrs. N.: Oh, I thought it was.

Sister A.: No, there was never trouble about that. They may have taken me off because I clipped the corner of the bus coming in the gate one night.

Q: They questioned your skill, huh?

Sister A.: Yes. I managed to do it, not when I was driving the nursery school children, but when I was driving a group of sisters home at night during retreat when they were supposed to be keeping silence. So I got off without a lot of comment from them. I didn't do much damage to the bus, and they should have removed those pillars a long time ago. One of the other delightful aspects of Daddy's association with the convent, I always think, was his comment to Admiral - Anderson? Can you identify him further?

Mrs. N.: I don't know who it was.

Sister A.: Whose daughter, Suki, had been in a convent.

Mrs. N.: Oh, yes. No, it was Captain Anderson.

Sister A.: Captain Anderson, who asked him once, I guess, how he felt about my being there, and Daddy explained that it was not a case of losing one daughter, it was a case of acquiring 345, which was certainly the case. He always displayed a tremendous interest in all of them.

Mrs. N.: They loved his stories.

Sister A.: They loved his stories and when he came - if he and Mother came alone and nobody happened to join the group, he was very quiet, for the most part. He would wander off to inspect the various trees he had had a part in planting. But if I had persuaded others to come along and sit down and they began asking him questions, he was absolutely at his best telling his stories. One of the funner stories about the tree-planting - I believe this was the day we planted the Pinus patula in front of Meadowland.

Mrs. N.: Yes.

Sister A.: Sister Bernadine, who had been previously so concerned about Commodore Grant as a "spy," came over. She was quite elderly at that time and walked with her cane and looked very frail. She came over with us to the planting of the pine tree and noticed a young Franciscan brother coming out of one of the buildings - in summer there's a summer school and they have all sorts of religious communities represented, both

Sister A. - 16

priests and brothers, and sisters - and she was determined that Daddy should see this Franciscan brother, particularly she wanted him to see his sandals, as I remember...

Mrs. N.: Yes, because he was barefooted with his sandals.

Sister A.: And to my rather great embarrassment, she insisted on my going over to get this young man and bringing him over to meet my father. I guess they had a good time when he got there, but I was most uneasy. I felt very foolish going over to ask him, you know, "Sister thinks my father should meet a Franciscan."

Q: What do they call them, discal...?

Sister A.: Well, he wasn't discalced. He had his sandals on. I think the discalced refers to shoeless, perhaps. I'm not sure, but I think maybe. But the Franciscans generally do wear sandals, and Sister Bernadine thought he was very picturesque. He was also a remarkably tolerant young man, I thought to accede to my mission.

Q: Your father wasn't particularly religious, however, himself, was he?

Mrs. N.: No, he certainly wasn't.

Sister A.: No, not in any formal sense, and yet if you look at his acts and occasionally, aren't there records of it in his speeches at various times?

Mrs. N.: Yes.

Sister A. - 17

Sister A.: To the dependence on God for success and for...

Q: His creed reminds me very much of General Eisenhower, who also had no real formal connections. He had one when he became president, but...

Mrs. N.: Well, I don't think anybody can take a fearful responsibility, such as Chester was faced with, without knowing that there are times when you've got to trust in God that you've made the right decision.

Sister A.: What about the time, Mother, that Daddy was in New York at the Darlington party, wasn't that it?

Mrs. N.: Oh, yes.

Sister A.: When Gilbert Darlington...

Mrs. N.: It was broadcasting.

Q: Heavenly Rest Darlington?

Mrs. N.: He was broadcasting. This was Captain Darlington.

Q: Wasn't he the onetime rector of Heavenly Rest?

Mrs. N.: No, that's his brother, isn't it? This is the one that was - he didn't preach in a church because he was quite deaf, but he was in the Naval Reserve.

Sister A.: And also, wasn't he president or associated with the American Bible Society in some way?

Mrs. N.: Yes. He was head of the American Bible Society at

Sister A. - 18

this time.

Sister A.: You tell the story, I don't know it well enough.

Mrs. N.: Well, he was in the business of this broadcast he made for Dr. Darlington and he remarked that he himself he didn't want to go under any false pretenses, that he himself did not go to church very much and then, in a moment of weakness, he said, "In fact, I don't know whether I've ever been baptized." This was a fatal remark to make in front of Dr. Darlington, who decided that Father must be baptized. Well, Father came home a very irate man, and he said "I won't be baptized. I think I probably was baptized." So I said, "Why don't you write back to Texas and ask them whether you have been baptized?" So he wrote to Texas, to one of his uncles, his uncle was a judge down there, and he said to this uncle, "and you needn't be too fussy about the sources, just be sure you find the records." So eventually the record came back, but in the meantime we were all just made Chester miserable, we all said, "Oh, life with Father, we're going to get Father baptized." And Chester would look at me and say, "If I get baptized, you're going to be baptized, too." I said, "I didn't shoot my mouth off in this situation. I'm not going to have anything to do with this." And Chester would keep saying to me, "I will not be baptized," and I would just start laughing and everybody in the family, Mary and everyone, would just shriek with laughter over this thing. Well, the thing came back and he had been baptized.

Sister A.: Lutheran, I guess? ~~Luther in the library.~~

Q: Probably his mother had seen to that, being a Lutheran.

Sister A.: Yes. Now I want to tell you, this illustrates what absolute impartiality Mother and Daddy had to the four of us. I believe – I am told, anyhow – when I was very small there was some Navy chaplain who wanted to baptize me, but I wasn't, I understand that the reason was that the other three hadn't been baptized and I was not going to have any special advantages. This came out when I had to find out, get prepared for when I was, indeed, baptized. Apparently, it hadn't been done before.

Q: You weren't actually baptized until you went into the convent? When you became a convert?

Sister A.: Right. I became a convert, oh, about 1950.

Mrs. N.: The other three are still unsaved.

Sister A.: I think they achieve plenty in good works for their salvation.

Q: That's a variant on Roman teaching.

Sister A.: Well, no. No..

Mrs. N.: Do unto others as you would be done unto. That's what we taught them all.

Sister A.: I don't know what their philosophical persuasions are in most cases, but as long as they are, well, unconvinced and standing by their own consciences. Even St. Thomas Aquinas says that if a man were to think, or to believe sincerely that Catholicism was wrong and he had been raised as such he would be obliged, in conscience, to stop practising it. So the conscience is supreme.

Q: Sister, in talking with your brother, he made this point very emphatically, that as he grew up he wasn't conscious so often of specific "thou shalt do this" and "thou shalt do that" on the part of his father, but he was very conscious of the fact that he was expected, and this was not expressed, but he was expected to measure up under all circumstances. He was expected to do the very best, and he was very conscious of the fact that his father set this example in terms of his naval career. Did you feel that, as a child growing up?

Sister A.: Well, I think we were always expected to produce to the utmost of our ability, and yet I do remember when I was not doing so well in the sixth grade that I never was scolded in any way for my performance. I brought home some liberal report cards filled with C's, I believe.

Mrs. N.: I don't remember your ever bringing home a report card with anything but a's on it.

Sister A.: I do remember there was a time - I think when I finally at Stanford brought home a c in descriptive astronomy perhaps it was, and Mother was so delighted because she finally realized she had a normal daughter.

Q: How did your father feel about it?

Sister A.: He never commented, as far as I know. He may never have known. Oh, one thing back. You asked me specifically about his religious feeling. He did have a prayer that he very much liked, and that was the one, "God, teach me to change the things that I can change, to accept the things that I cannot change, and the wisdom to know the difference." You see that written commonly.

Mrs. N.: He'd always believed that.

Q: That's one of the favorites..

Sister A.: I often did wonder, especially toward the end when he was so sick, what his attitude toward suffering was precisely. Whether he thought of it strictly as something to be endured as contributing to growth in character, perhaps, or whether he thought of it as more...

Mrs. N.: I think he just thought of it actually as a pain in the neck.

Q: Just a kind of an affliction.

Mrs. N.: Something that kept him from doing what he wanted to do.

Q: Did he have a belief in an afterlife?

Mrs. N.: No, I don't know that he did. I dont' think he ever expressed it. His idea, and, I think, my idea is do the very

Sister A. - 22

best you can in this life. You don't know what's ahead of you, but if there's anything, that's lovely. But if there isn't you will have achieved what you set out to do, or come near it, if you do your very level best.

Q: This is faith, isn't it?

Mrs. N.: It is faith. A complete faith.

Sister A.: One of Daddy's interventions in community life, shall we say, occurred on March 11, 1945, when I had been asked to christen the USS Buck, which was a destroyer, here in San Francisco. Being able to invite a certain number of people that I would like to have come, out of courtesy, I wanted to invite some of the sisters, even though I knew that, according to the regulations, they could not come. It was a public function, and they were not supposed to be at those things in those days. Now they more or less consider it a public duty.

Q: This was at 8 o'clock in the morning.

Sister A.: Yes, it was at 8 o'clock in the morning, and the night before Catherine - wasn't it the night before?

Mrs. N.: What?

Sister A.: That Catherine was being married on the East Coast?

Q: Mrs. Lay?

Mrs. N.: Yes, well we had to be on the East Coast, and we said we hoped to get back in time for the christening, but if we don't, we turned to the young aide of Admiral Greenslade, and said, "You are it. You look out for Mary."

Sister A.: So he sent for me in the early morning - oh, yes, and when Daddy did enquire at one point whether or not the sisters were going to be able to come, and it must have been Mother Margaret or Mother Justin at that time...

Mrs. N.: Mother Margaret.

Sister A.: Mother Margaret - was mother general, and she said, no, it was not permissible, and Daddy took it up with the archbishop, and they came.

Q: He always had that advantage, didn't he?

Sister A.: Yes.

Q: How did that effect you, as a child, the fact that you knew your father had access to the very highest authority.

Mrs. N.: He never used - let the children feel that he had it.

Sister A.: And, I don't know about the others, but I sure never used it. I remember...

Mrs. N.: No - the children, not one of them would use it.

Sister A.: As a matter of fact, I think more often than not I'd be inclined - oh, the answer is, I did the night before the Nimitz Day in Washington, D.C., or I wouldn't speak as I did in asking the principal's permission to be excused from classes.

Sister A. - 24

Q: Tell me that story.

Sister A.: Yes. When this day was coming up and I knew I was going to participate -

Q: That was in '45?

Sister A.: In '45, October 5th. The day before I went to the principal or dean of students, whichever it was, and asked for permission to be excused from classes the next day because my father was coming home, saying a little more than that. And then, also, during that time in Washington, I remember I had to go down to the Naval Dispensary for something - I guess it was that annual x-ray - and I forget how I got down there, but it must have been a combination of bus and walking - and I checked in just as anybody else did, and I waited a good three hours and forty-five minutes. When they read on my dependent's card to whom I was related, they were most appalled at having kept me waiting for so long, but I didn't think anything of it, and I think that none of us ever tried to pull rank or were a bit pushy about it. I think we all wanted to be - we were proud of Daddy in every way, but we wanted to be known for ourselves, for our own worth, rather than specifically as being related to him.

Q: This certainly speaks volumes about training in the home.

Sister A.: I think so. It's not one's connections that make one's worth, but strictly what one's self produces.

Sister A. - 25

Q: This ties in so closely with his attitude that you had to measure up.

Sister A.: Yes. One other incident from the - well, it happened more than once - in Washington, D.C.. This was one of the consequences of growing up in a Navy family, I figure. Admiral Robison used to come and visit periodically.

Q: Is he...?

Mrs. N.: S.S. Robison.

Sister A.: And it just so happened sometimes that Mother and Daddy had a previous engagement outward. Well, I was left at home to entertain Admiral Robison, and it was a little - well, he was talkative enough himself, but when I once told him that I was studying Marmion in English, I got thereafter quoted yards and yards of Marmion at me during my meal.

Q: So you avoided that subject?

Sister A.: Yes. Also in Washington, D.C. - now, you understand that we, the four of us children, had some of the same faults that every family does, some of the same self-interest of children, and when it came to getting Daddy a birthday present once, we got him a badminton set, which he I think never used, but we used often. We tried playing it outside on the grounds of the Naval Observatory, but we found it was far too windy for that, so we would play it in the main living room.

Mrs. N.: In the foyer.

Sister A. - 26

Sister A.: And to the great peril of this huge glass mirror that stood over the mantel, and the back swing of a racket. Another thing that Daddy was always most interested in was our musical ability. He enjoyed listening to music, although his knowledge of it in the formal sense was probably practically nil.

Q: Did he play any instrument?

Sister A.: No.

Q: Did he sing?

Mrs. N.: No, he sort of hummed along. He just loved music.

Sister A.: He loved music and had a wonderful collection of records, and always was very interested when the four of us played. And this is another interest which the family fostered. Every one of us played at least one instrument.

Q: So you had a sort of a toy symphony?

Sister A.: Kind of, yes. One time when I went back East, it was Christmas of 1949, I guess, just after I had started at Stanford, I went back East at Christmas time. I wanted to use a check I had gotten for Christmas to buy a recorder flute. Nancy had a soprano recorder and we wanted to get an alto recorder. Kate already had the tenor. Chet played the violin.

Mrs. N.: Franny the cello, Katherine the piano - Catherine had played the viola. The viola was my instrument in addition to

Sister A. - 27

a piano, which I had ~~been brought up into~~ *learned while growing up.(?)* — I inherited Kate's viola from her...

Q: My, what a set of musicians.

Sister A.: ...and after I'd bought the flute - recorder, rather - I was also looking around for some music. Nancy was there with me, and we found this one book of Elizabethan airs, which was scored for violin, viola, cello, and all four recorders. We were just thrilled, because we could play it all within the family. Then we realized to our horror, yes, but some of us would have to play two instruments.

Q: You remind me a bit of the Trapp family.

Sister A.: There was something funny that something I just said there reminded me of. I wish I could think of it.

Mrs. N.: The what?

Sister A.: There was something I said in that sequence that reminded me of something else, but it escapes me now. Oh, musical ability. Mother, tell about the "evening" Daddy conducted the San Francisco Symphony.

Mrs. N.: I've forgotten about that.

Sister A.: The dream..

Mrs. N.: Oh, yes. I can't remember it, though.

Sister A.: You woke up because he was thrashing so violently, and you finally woke him up, and he was in an absolute sweat

Sister A. - 28

because he had been thrust out on the stage of the San Francisco Opera House to conduct the San Francisco Symphony, and his line, "and I didn't even have a score." As if he could have read it, had he had it! You remember that?

Mrs. N.: Yes, I do.

Q: Was that at the time he was being so interested in the...

Sister A.: In the symphony, yes.

Mrs. N.: I had been on the symphony board for years, and we used to go to the symphony every single week, and he loved the symphony, and knew all the conductors and all the people in the symphony and all. And to the very end - well, the last year he didn't go to the symphony because he wasn't well enough - but otherwise we went constantly, and he just dearly loved symphony music. But not modern symphony music.

Q: What about opera, was he fond of that?

Mrs. N.: We went to the opera a good deal, yes, but he was not as fond of the opera as he was of the symphony. But he and dear Mrs. Ehrman - or Mrs. Sigmund Stern - would always sit in the back of the opera box and sleep.

Sister A.: One of the more recent memories is the time that Daddy and Mother came down to Stanford to visit. We had been alerted ahead of time, and this time they were coming to the college itself to see 420B, which was the room in which I and other graduate students were working under Dr. Geiser, my major professor, all had study cubicles (?). We were a very lively group and they were all interested in meeting Daddy. Oh, may be I should stop here. There's another very funny story in connection with that. When I first went down to Stanford in the PhD program, I first had to register with my family name, but within the department I was just Sister Aquinas, and Dr. Geisc knew my relationship to Daddy, but none of the others did, and I guess somewhere along the way it began to dribble in. I was in my cubicle one day eating my lunch, because at that time sisters were not yet permitted to eat with everybody else, and the rest of them were sitting outside, and I don't know that they knew I was there. Oh, yes, I guess they did, but they were discussing, and one of them, the boy from across the hall had come in and he had heard this, and he was asking, was it so. And they said, oh yes, yes, it was so, that Admiral Nimitz was my father. The boy couldn't believe it, and so they finally had to refer the question through the air into the cubicle and ask me. I said, yes, that was so.

Anyhow, Daddy came this particular day and it was during the football season, and he had the unparalleled gall of coming as a regent of the University of California with a gold and blue tie on, which the students duly commented on. He had a streak of mischief. I would say some of the earlier stories I heard from him, which I'm sure you must have records of - the beer party back at the Naval Academy?

Mrs. N.: Oh, yes.

Q: No. Tell me, I don't know that.

Sister A.: Eller must have it. I sent it to him. I know I did. He and a group of his cohorts had decided to throw a beer party, and it fell to his lot to be the one to procure the beer. He couldn't do this directly - this is strictly verboten - and I guess they always had to wear their uniforms...

Mrs. N.: Yes. And they weren't allowed to buy it.

Sister A.: So he went - as a first class man he had all the privileges to go in and out of the gate/any time he wanted...

Mrs. N.: To have his uniform fitted.

Sister A.: To have his uniform fitted out, that's right, because this was very near the end of his time. He went to the tailor's and got - I guess one of the tailor's assistants to perform this little task

Mrs. N.: Well, he said to the tailor, he just threw the suitcase down, he saw there was a man there in civilian clothes, he didn't pay any attention to him, he said, "Fill this with beer, will you?' Then he went out, and he came back and got it.

Sister A.: Yes, he had the beer, and so Daddy took the beer back to the place and they had a wonderful time. Apparently in the place - was it Bancroft Hall, where they had this?

Mrs. N.: Yes.

Sister A. - 31

Sister A.: There was a roof area which could not be seen from any other window, but they were making sufficient noise that they could see the guards disturbed knowing that there was something going on somewhere. What did they call them, jimmy legs?

Mrs. N.: Yes.

Sister A.: Something like that. Sort of stirring about down below, uneasy because of this unusual amount of noise. They'd had a marvelous party, and the next Monday morning, Daddy marched his company into class and, to his horror, there the new professor on the platform was this man he'd seen in civilian clothes at the tailor's. Well, he had a very uneasy class, and he said he had many uneasy classes the next few days, but nothing happened. It was just as he was graduating, and he was in the midshipman rank. He was a four or five striper, wasn't he?

Mrs. N.: I think he may have been a three-striper.

Sister A.: Something of that sort. Anyhow, he was just horribly uneasy...

Q: He could see catastrophe ahead.

Mrs. N.: But he never batted an eyelash.

Sister A.: Never batted an eyelash, and Daddy said that from this incident he learned to be lenient always with first offenders. Daddy said he also learned that he would never play

Sister A. - 32

fast and loose with the regulations again. Several years later, when he figured it was safe to do so, he tried to look up the man to thank him for the lesson, and found that the man had already died, I believe.

Mrs. N.: It was Commander Bertolet. He had been a commander on the Vermont when we knew him. And he had died down at Guayaquil, so he didn't have a chance to thank him.

Q: Sister, your father is known by everybody to never have said anything derogatory about people. He may have had strong feelings about a certain person, but he never, in public, at least, said anything derogatory. This is really a very Christian attitude, isn't it?

Sister A.: There is another aspect of it, a *particular* area of it, was the fact that no matter what he thought, went on inactive duty, of the action, say, of either the president or anybody, either a general or admiral, any officer in the service of the government, you could never get him to criticize. You never heard him criticize it. As a matter of fact, if you asked him what he thought of it, you might get the slightest *tinge* that he didn't agree, but he would always say, "We have to support the decision" or the attitude, or the - there was very much a feeling of complete loyalty in that regard, which, of course, rubbed off on those around, I think. Loyalty to superiors.

Q: That has a special bearing with you, doesn;t it?

Sister A. - 33

Sister A.: Yes, very much so. One of the interesting things Admiral Eller has established at our library - Archbishop Alamany Library - at the college, a Nimitz collection. It was originally a collection of naval history and I can't even remember now how the thing got started.

Q: Well he sends to each one of the children - he sends all the historical documents.

Sister A.: But he sent me a great deal more. He sent me — *he obtained* some old books, old text books of naval history, to give to the library. One of the books he sent was Admiral - the biography of Admiral Spruance, put out by the Division of Naval History in Washington, D.C. and I forget, Forester?

Mrs. N.: Admiral Raymond A. Spruance.

Sister A.: Yes, but who was the author of it?

Mrs. N.: Oh, it was one of the people on Spruance's staff.

Sister A.: And the sub-title was "A study in Command" or "Command Personality", or something like that.

Mrs. N.: Admiral Forrestal.

Sister A.: Forrestal.

Mrs. N.: And the forward is by Chester.

Sister A.: I was most interested in that book because one of the aspects brought out in it was his skill as a commander, his technique, so to speak, of leadership. And so much that is

Sister A. - 34

true in military service,—where obedience must be absolute, is also applicable to a religious life, where obedience should be absolute. It's not the fate of a nation that depends on it but it certainly is a matter of peace and harmony.

Q: The fate of the community.

Sister A.: The fate of the community which depends on it, and the individual's own happiness. I've always felt that from studying people in the army and the Navy, who were great leaders, religious superiors could gain a great insight into techniques of leadership. I found that book was immensely interesting.

Q: That's an interesting insight.

Sister A.: Oh, I know. There was also that article which I'm sure Eller must have, called, "My Life, the U.S. Navy" that appeared in <u>Boys' Life</u>, and it was actually Daddy's words as told to somebody else. In there he brought out the idea of loyalty up, loyalty down. If you do your best to give the people under you everything they need to work with to do a good job for you, you'll have their loyalty, and it's your loyalty to them that makes you give them all the support that they need.

Q: This came right out of his life.

Sister A.: Right out of his life, and another tremendously, I think, important idea transferred from military service into religious life.

Sister A. 35

Mrs. N.: This is an interesting conception, isn't it?

Q: Yes, it is.

Sister A.: Well, you know, Ignatius of Loyola and the Jesuit Order are spoken of as the Army of Jesus Christ, and Ignatius himself was a soldier, before he became a founder of a religious order, and I imagine a great deal of what he learned in one sphere transferred to another.

Q: Well, in baptism itself, you're baptized into the...

Sister A.: Right, into a Christian army.

Q: Yes. Tell me more about your father's sense of humor. This also has its application in the religious community, but talk about it in terms of him, as you remember him.

Sister A.: Yes. It was unfailing, and he was never more at home, I don't think, than when he was telling a good story. Oh, one time, we played a little trick on him. He always used to tease me because my eyesight's not too good. He used to tease me about looking from Berkeley out to the Golden Gate Bridge, about being able to read the newspaper over people's shoulders with a great big pair of Japanese binoculars that had been captured off some Japanese ship. One night - and I can't remember what prompted it - we were sitting in the little sort of breakfast room having our supper and looking out over the Bay, and it was evening and time for a new moon, about, and I looked out and there was no new moon out there. But I said something about the tiniest little sliver of a moon out there. And Mother took it up with me, and we had him really uncomfortable because he couldn't see it. We paid him back for all the times he'd teased me about the things I couldn't see. I think he was vastly relieved.

Mrs. N.: Tell him about Dad's love of using his - he had a finger off. Tell him about what he'd do with children.

Sister A.: Oh, yes. Daddy was minus the fourth finger of his left hand...

Q: Which was a naval accident, wasn't it?

Sister A.: Yes. Wasn't it an accident with building the engines...

Mrs. N.: The engine for the Maumee. He would capitalize on this shortened finger when playing with children, and he would horrify them by putting his finger all the way into his ear, you know, to the middle of his head, by making his finger disappear, by playing a trick on them and substituting a whole finger for a half, and they were not quick enough to catch it.

Mrs. N.: He just loved that.

Sister A.: He entertained children for hours that way, and also with card stunts. He was a very good card stunt player.

Mrs. N.: He used to do all kinds of magic tricks. He loved it, and, oh, he would get the children absolutely frantic.

Sister A. - 37

Sister A.: There's one marvelous little picture of him with a group of children down at the Nimitz School in Cupertino. They're all around him and he's obviously just enjoying it immensely, just with expressions of delight and awe, mixed. I wish I could think of more of his favorite stories. The ones I would be deign to tell him.

Q: The ones which you, as a religious, could tell me.

Sister A.: Would be willing to repeat.

Q: Your brother says that he used to tell so many stories about his boyhood and that your mother sometimes suspected that they were apocryphal.

Mrs. N.: Chester could really make a very good story, and I can give you a lot of his stories because I kept those on tap.

Q: Good. I shall look forward to them.

Mrs. N.: He had a lot of excellent stories.

Q: Will you repeat those two stories for me now, the one about the cake and the one about the soil.

Mrs. N.: At one period during the war, the Admiral received a letter from a mother of one of the soldiers out in his area, and she said that her boy had always had a birthday cake, and would the Admiral go to the nearest bakery and take the five dollars she was enclosing, and have a birthday cake made. Well, the nearest bakery was a good many thousand miles away.

Sister A.: She called it a bakeshop, Mother.

Mrs. N.: A bakeshop, yes, but the bakeshop was quite a distance off. He had the cake made and then had it sent to the boy in his unit. She was very pleased over this, and the boy was extremely pleased.

Q: I would think he would be.

Mrs. N.: Then another mother sent him a bag, perhaps a ? sand box bag, of Mississippi soil, saying her son said if he could only get his feet in Mississippi soil, he'd be happy. So the Admiral found out what company the boy was in and then sent it to his commanding officer, telling him to put the soil around the flagpole, and have all the Mississippi boys in his company come, remove their shoes and socks, and walk through this soil, which they did.

Sister A.: There's still another story which illustrates his sense of humor - and, well, heart. I understand that while he was still at Pearl Harbor, some sailor got in to see him one day, who said that he had come strictly on a bet from his cohorts back in the barracks that he couldn't - the others had bet him that he'd never get in to see Admiral Nimitz. That he wasn't accessible, and the boy said he was and he was going to go. So when he got in there and he met Daddy, Daddy said, well, now, how are you going to prove it to them that you were here? And I guess that had the boy a bit puzzled, but Daddy sent for a photographer to establish the record.

Mrs. N.: He had his picture taken with this boy.

Q: All of these do say something about his sense of humor, but they also say something about his awareness of good public relations.

Sister A.: Oh, yes, two other stories, Mother. Norma Day.

Mrs. N.: Yes, tell him about that.

Sister A.: You know those letters better than I do.

Mrs. N.: Well, anyway, this little girl wrote to Chester when he was in the Pacific and she said, "I am so sorry, Admiral, that you weren't here today, because my family were expecting the threshing crew, and my mother had legs of lamb, beef roasts, and chicken, and turkey, and all kinds of pies ready, and then the weather turned bad and they couldn't come. If you were just here you could have had anything you wanted." Well, the Admiral began answering this little girl's letter, and the conversation became very interesting indeed, and it was carried on all through the war.

Q: The correspondence?

Mrs. N.: Yes, the correspondence was carried on, and after the war he still wrote to this girl, and then he was sent by the United Nations out to, I think it was DesMoines, Iowa, and he said he would come out and accept the task of giving a speech, but he asked if the family of Norma Day, telling them where they lived, could be invited in to spend the day with him, and to be his special guests. So they were invited in, and Norma Day's farmer father, her mother, and her brother, and Norma came in, and were in the same carriage with Admiral Nimitz in all the processions and the - when he made the speeches and all. This was a great thrill for them to meet him in person, and he said they were a delightful family.

Soon after the Admiral had to fly out somewhere over Iowa, so he sent word to Norma "You watch for me, when my plane goes over, because we'll go over your house and I'll drop you something." And I had bought a very lovely scarf for her, and he had a little parachute made, and this was to be dropped, but he got over Iowa the clouds were so thick, they had no idea where the house was, so he had to take it all the way to San Diego and mail it back.

Sister A.: Another funny incident - or funny series of incidents were the postcards from the astrologer up in northern - was it Washington?

Mrs.N.: Seattle, I think. He told him what the weather was going to be, and also he said, there is a little island in the Pacific that is known to no one but myself, and he said, I will tell you where it is. If you could take that island, and then he went on this way, and that way about it, and the Admiral had the satisfaction of writing back to him and saying we took that island a long time ago.

Sister A. - 41

Mrs. N.

...down from Berkeley, we'd both driven down and both my son-in-law, "Junior" Lay, was living there and Chester was living there. They were living quite close together, and we were spending time with both of them. And in this particular instance - it was Christmas Eve - and Mary had come down from the convent. She was not yet a nun, she was just at school there, and we were having Christmas Eve over at my son's house. It was just before he was sent to Korea. My husband made some statement, and for a long time nobody had corrected the Admiral or changed his remarks, you see. They listened with awe. He was quite used to making statements and people accepted them. Well, this time my son-in-law had been a young ensign out of Annapolis, and his first ship was the Augusta, which my husband commanded. So he had trained this young ensign the way he should go. The other one, his son, had been trained from childhood up until he went into the Naval Academy by his father, and on this particular evening, they were all talking as they were setting and unsetting the table and so on and so forth, and my husband made a comment, and to my absolute amusement, both his son-in-law and his son said, "Daddy, that's not right. It isn't the way it is now." Chester looked very startled and then he looked at me, and I had a twinkle in my eye and was laughing. Then these two sat down by their father and each one was saying, "Now, Daddy, it's this way. Daddy, I tell you..." and they went on with this conversation. It was the first time, I think, that anybody in a number of years had suggested to Chester that perhaps he wasn't absolutely in touch with what was going on. These two were so delighted and when Chester went home, he laughed all the way home. He thought this was terribly funny. That his two sons were the ones to tell him off.

INDEX

for an interview

with

SISTER MARY AQUINAS (NIMITZ)

Anderson, Captain E. Robert, 14-15

Archbishop Alamany Library, 33

Arizona, 3

Augusta, 2, 41

Battha, Maria, Magda, Margit, and Marta, 11-12

Bede, Sister, 7-8

Berkeley, 3

Bernadine, Sister, 7, 15-16

Bertolet, Commander Levi Calvin, 32

Buck, 22

Calhoun, Admiral William Lowndes, 5

Childhood, (Mary's) 1-11

Darlington, Captain Gilbert, 17-18

Day, Norma, 39-40

Ehrman, Mrs., 28

Eisenhower, General Dwight D., 17

Eller, Admiral E. M., 30, 33-34

Forrestel, Admiral Emmet Peter, 33

Franny, 26

Geise, Dr., 28-29

Greenslade, Admiral John Wills, 23

Hirase, Shintaro, 6

Lay, Junior, 41

Margaret, Mother, 23

Maumee, 36

Naval Academy, 29-31

Nimitz, Catherine, 22, 26-27

Nimitz, Chester Jr., 26

Nimitz, Nancy, 26

Religion, 18-19, 21-22

Robison, Admiral S. S., 25

Shafroth, John Franklin, 4

Spruance, Admiral Raymond Ames, 33

Stern, Mrs. Sigmund, 28

Vermont, 32

www.ingramcontent.com/pod-product-compliance
Lightning Source LLC
Chambersburg PA
CBHW080614170426
43209CB00007B/1433